MAYER SMITH

The Man Who Lived Inside a Poem

First edition

This book was professionally typeset on Reedsy.
Find out more at reedsy.com

Contents

1

The Mysterious Manuscript

The bell above the shop door tinkled faintly as Evan pushed it open, stepping into the dim, dusty embrace of the old bookstore. The scent of aging paper and leather bindings wrapped around him, comforting and familiar. He'd wandered into countless shops like this over the years, chasing whispers of inspiration for his faltering poetry. But tonight, something felt different— off, even.

The shopkeeper, a hunched figure with spectacles perched precariously on the edge of her nose, looked up briefly from her desk. She gave a small, almost imperceptible nod before returning her attention to the thick ledger in front of her.

Evan meandered through the narrow aisles, his fingers brushing over spines that bore titles ranging from the mundane to the arcane. He wasn't sure what he was looking for—he rarely was—but the weight in his chest told him something waited here. His boots scuffed against the uneven wooden floorboards, the sound unnervingly loud in the otherwise silent shop.

In the back corner of the store, a single beam of moonlight spilled through a crack in the ceiling, illuminating a small wooden table. On it sat a book, as though deliberately placed there for him to find. The manuscript was bound in worn, black leather, its edges frayed and delicate. No title adorned the cover, no hint of what lay within.

Drawn inexplicably to it, Evan reached out, his hand hovering over the cover. The air around the book seemed warmer, almost pulsing with a life of its own. His fingertips brushed the leather, and a shiver ran up his arm. He hesitated, glancing over his shoulder toward the shopkeeper, who now seemed oddly still, her head bowed over the ledger as though asleep.

When he opened the book, the pages were yellowed with age, their texture soft under his fingertips. The handwriting was elegant yet uneven, the ink faint in places, as if written in haste. What caught his attention first, however, wasn't the poetic lines scattered across the page—it was his name.

Evan.

It wasn't a name he expected to see in an old manuscript. He blinked, certain his eyes were playing tricks on him, but there it was again, scrawled in the margins of a verse:

"To Evan, whose path is yet unwritten."

His heart thudded against his ribs. He flipped through the pages, scanning hurriedly. Each verse seemed more cryptic than the last—vivid imagery of shadows and light, of lovers lost and found, of places that felt hauntingly familiar despite being entirely unknown to him.

Toward the back of the book, he found another note:
   "This manuscript belongs to those who dare to live within its words."

The lights in the shop flickered, pulling Evan out of the trance-like state the book had cast over him. He looked around, suddenly aware of how still and quiet the store had become. The shopkeeper was gone.

"Hello?" Evan called, his voice barely rising above a whisper.

No response.

The door to the shop was ajar, though he didn't remember hearing it open. A chill crept through the crack, and with it came the faintest sound—a whisper. At first, he thought it was the wind, but the longer he listened, the clearer it became. The whisper wasn't outside; it was coming from the manuscript.

He stared at the book in his hands, his breath shallow. The words on the page shimmered, rearranging themselves before his eyes. His pulse quickened as a new verse emerged:
   "The seeker's truth lies hidden deep;
   Through verse and shadow, secrets seep."

The whisper grew louder, the words faint but persistent, repeating the verse over and over. Evan slammed the book shut, but the sound didn't stop.

He bolted for the door, clutching the manuscript tightly against his chest. The cold night air hit him like a wall as he stumbled out into the deserted street. The shop behind him was dark now, its windows lifeless, the bell above the door silent.

Evan turned back, his hands trembling as he stared at the manuscript. For the first time, he noticed faint etchings on the leather cover, almost like a title scratched out of existence. But one word remained clear at the center of it all:

"Begin."

2

The Enigma of Ella

Evan's apartment was a cramped sanctuary of chaos: shelves overflowing with books, half-filled notebooks piled on the desk, and coffee-stained scraps of paper scattered like autumn leaves. But that night, it felt oppressive, every shadow in the dimly lit room seemingly alive with secrets. The manuscript sat on the small table by the window, its black leather cover glinting faintly in the glow of the streetlamp outside.

He hadn't dared to open it again since leaving the bookstore. The words it had whispered still lingered in his mind, elusive yet unsettling, like a song he couldn't place but couldn't stop hearing. He sipped his now-cold coffee, staring at the book as though it might leap at him.

A knock at the door shattered the silence.

Evan froze, the cup slipping from his hands and clattering onto the floor. It was nearly midnight—no one visited him at this hour. His pulse quickened as the knock came again, louder this time.

"Who is it?" he called, his voice unsteady.

"Ella," a woman replied, her tone calm yet edged with urgency.

He frowned. He didn't know an Ella—or did he? The name stirred something deep within him, a faint echo of familiarity.

He approached the door cautiously, his fingers brushing against the chain lock. "What do you want?"

"I need to talk to you. About the manuscript," she said, her voice muffled but clear.

Evan's breath caught. The manuscript? How could she know about it? His hand lingered on the lock, indecision paralyzing him.

"I don't have time to explain out here," she continued, as if sensing his hesitation. "Please, just let me in. It's important."

Against his better judgment, he slid the chain free and opened the door.

Ella stood in the dim hallway, her figure partially silhouetted by the flickering light above. She was striking, with piercing green eyes that seemed to hold secrets of their own. Her dark hair fell in loose waves around her shoulders, and she clutched a leather satchel tightly against her side.

"Can I come in?" she asked, her gaze darting past him into the apartment, as though scanning for something—or someone.

Evan stepped aside reluctantly, allowing her to enter. She moved with a quiet intensity, her eyes immediately landing on the manuscript sitting on the table.

"You've read it," she said, more a statement than a question.

"Who are you?" Evan demanded, closing the door behind her.

Ella turned to face him, her expression unreadable. "Someone who's been looking for that book for a very long time."

"That doesn't answer my question."

She sighed, placing her satchel on the floor. "My name is Ella. Let's just say the manuscript and I... have a history."

Evan crossed his arms. "What kind of history?"

She hesitated, her gaze dropping to the floor. "The kind that doesn't usually end well."

Her words sent a chill through him. "Why are you here?"

"Because you've already started," she said, her voice soft but firm. "The moment you opened that book, you became part of its story. And that makes you a target."

"A target for what?"

"For the ones who want it back," she said simply, as though that explained everything.

Evan shook his head, disbelief mixing with frustration. "This is insane. I don't even know what this thing is, let alone why anyone would want it."

"You will," Ella said cryptically. She stepped closer to the manuscript, her fingers hovering just above its cover. "Do you know what this book is capable of?"

"No," he admitted, his voice barely a whisper.

"It's not just a collection of poetry," she said. "It's a gateway. A map. And a trap, if you're not careful."

Her words made his stomach churn. "A gateway to what?"

"To a world written in ink and bound by verse," she replied. "But it's not a place you can visit without consequence. The manuscript chooses who it pulls in, and it doesn't let go easily."

Evan felt the room spin slightly as her words sank in. "You're telling me this... thing is alive?"

"In a way," Ella said. "It's tied to whoever writes in it, and to whoever reads it. And now, it's tied to you."

Before Evan could respond, the lights in the apartment flickered. Both of them turned toward the window, where the streetlamp outside dimmed, then went out entirely.

"They're here," Ella whispered, her voice tense.

"Who's here?" Evan asked, panic rising in his chest.

Ella didn't answer. Instead, she reached into her satchel and pulled out a small, leather-bound journal. She opened it quickly, flipping to a specific page.

"Stay behind me," she said, her tone leaving no room for argument.

The air in the room grew heavy, a faint hum resonating just below the edge of hearing. Shadows began to shift unnaturally along the walls, pooling together like ink spilled on paper. Evan's heart pounded as the manuscript on the table seemed to thrum in response, its leather cover vibrating faintly.

Ella began to recite something under her breath, her words quick and lyrical, as though weaving a spell. The shadows recoiled slightly, but not entirely. One began to take shape, stretching upward into a humanoid form, its edges flickering like the flame of a dying candle.

"Get away from the book," Ella commanded, her voice rising with authority.

The shadow hesitated, then lunged forward. Ella slammed her hand down on the manuscript, shouting a single word that echoed unnaturally in the room. The shadow dissolved into nothingness, leaving a cold, empty silence behind.

Evan collapsed into the nearest chair, his legs trembling. "What the hell was that?"

Ella turned to him, her face pale but determined. "A warning," she said. "We don't have much time. If you want to survive this, you'll have to trust me."

Evan stared at her, his mind racing with questions he wasn't sure he wanted answered. For the first time in years, he felt like a character in someone else's story—and he wasn't sure if it would end well.

3

Whispers in Verse

Evan barely slept. When he did, it wasn't restful. Dreams tugged at his consciousness, vivid and strange, as if stitched together from scraps of someone else's memories. He wandered through darkened corridors lined with endless bookshelves, their volumes whispering unintelligible words. Shadows lurked just beyond the periphery of his vision, and each step forward felt like sinking into wet ink.

He awoke with a gasp, the taste of metallic fear sharp in his mouth. The first rays of dawn filtered through the blinds, casting slanted lines across his disheveled room. The manuscript sat on his desk, closed but still emanating an inexplicable presence, like a sleeping predator.

Ella was gone. Sometime during the night, she'd left without a word, though the faint scent of her perfume lingered in the air. On the table beside the manuscript, she'd left her leather-bound journal, open to a page filled with hurriedly scribbled notes.

Evan rubbed his eyes and leaned closer to read:

"The ink whispers truth. Beware the verse that binds. Seek the Seeker's Door."

Beneath it, in smaller writing, was a single stanza:
    "Under the moonlight's weary gaze,
    A path of shadows, a mind's malaise.
    Beyond the veil where secrets keep,
    The Seeker waits in eternal sleep."

He frowned, the words twisting uncomfortably in his mind, as if they held a weight beyond their meaning. Something about them felt familiar, though he couldn't place why.

As he stared at the page, a faint sound reached his ears—a whisper, so soft it could have been mistaken for the wind. It grew louder, the words still indistinct, until he realized they weren't coming from outside. They were coming from the manuscript.

Evan hesitated, his heart pounding. Every instinct told him to leave it alone, to walk away. But the pull of curiosity was stronger. Slowly, he reached out and opened the book.

The pages flipped on their own, the rustling sound unnervingly like dry laughter. They stopped midway through, revealing a blank sheet. At first, he saw nothing, but then faint words began to form, as if being written by an invisible hand:

"Evan... do you dare to follow?"

He swallowed hard. The whispering grew louder, the words now distinct but in a language he didn't recognize. The script on the page shimmered, shifting into an image—a dark forest illuminated by a pale moon. The scene was so vivid it seemed to pulse with life, the shadows between the trees writhing as though alive.

A sharp knock at the window startled him. Evan whipped his head around, his breath caught in his throat. Outside, standing motionless on the sidewalk, was a man in a long coat. His face was obscured by the brim of a wide hat, but Evan could feel the weight of his gaze.

The knock came again, louder this time, though the man hadn't moved. Evan backed away from the desk, the manuscript still open and humming softly.

Another knock, this time at the door.

"Evan?" a voice called.

It wasn't Ella. It was deeper, unfamiliar, and edged with something sharp.

Evan's pulse quickened. He didn't answer.

The knocking grew more insistent. "Evan, we know you have it. Open the door."

He glanced back at the manuscript, the image of the forest still vivid on the page. The whispering from the book began to harmonize with the voice at the door, creating a strange, discordant melody.

Without thinking, Evan grabbed Ella's journal and the manuscript, shoving them into his bag. The knocking turned into pounding, the door rattling in its frame.

"Evan!" the voice shouted, now furious.

The lights flickered, and shadows began to seep under the door like black smoke. Evan panicked, looking toward the window. The man in the coat was gone.

With no other option, Evan yanked the window open and climbed out onto the fire escape. The cold morning air hit him like a slap, but he didn't stop. He clutched the bag to his chest as he descended, his breath visible in frantic puffs.

When he reached the alley below, the world was eerily quiet. The pounding on his apartment door had stopped. He glanced up at his window, but the room was dark.

A soft rustle behind him made him spin around. Standing at the mouth of the alley was the man in the coat. His face was still obscured, but now Evan could see his hands—long, pale fingers stained with what looked like ink.

Evan took a step back.

"Don't run," the man said, his voice smooth and unsettling. "You won't get far."

Ignoring him, Evan turned and bolted. He sprinted through the empty streets, the buildings around him seeming to blur as he ran. The bag thumped against his side with every step, the weight of the manuscript feeling heavier with each passing second.

When he finally stopped, gasping for air, he found himself in a part of the city he didn't recognize. The streets were narrower, the buildings older, their windows darkened as though abandoned. The sound of his own breathing echoed unnaturally.

The whispering returned, louder now, and distinctly coming from the bag. Evan hesitated, then pulled out the manuscript. The image of the forest on the page had changed. Now, it showed a single tree with a door carved into its trunk.

Beneath it, new words had appeared:
   "Enter the verse. Find the Seeker."

Before Evan could react, the air around him grew heavy, and the shadows of the alley stretched toward him, their edges razor-sharp. The last thing he heard before everything went black was the man's voice, distant and mocking:

"Welcome to the story."

4

The Seeker's Door

Evan's eyes fluttered open to find himself lying on cold, uneven ground. His head throbbed with a dull ache, and the taste of copper lingered in his mouth. His limbs felt heavy, as if weighed down by invisible chains, but as he pushed himself into a sitting position, the pain receded slightly, leaving only the dizzying sense of displacement.

He wasn't in the alley anymore. The oppressive, claustrophobic air of the city had vanished, replaced by something far stranger. The ground beneath him was not concrete or asphalt but soft, damp earth. He could smell the rich scent of moss and decay in the air, and around him stretched a vast, eerie forest. The trees were ancient, their trunks gnarled and twisted like the limbs of some forgotten creature. Thick, hanging vines draped from the branches, creating a canopy that obscured most of the sky. A faint mist clung to the ground, swirling like ghostly tendrils as the wind whispered through the trees.

The only sound was the distant rustle of leaves, and his own breath, coming in shallow, uneven gasps.

He scrambled to his feet, eyes scanning the shadowy surround-
ings. The forest felt alive—watchful. Every time he thought he
saw something move out of the corner of his eye, it vanished
before he could focus on it.

"Where am I?" he muttered, his voice unnaturally loud in the
silence.

His hand instinctively reached for the bag at his side, and the
manuscript pressed against him like a living thing, its presence
undeniable. With a trembling hand, he pulled it out, the pages
almost humming in his grasp, as if calling to him. The image
of the tree from before—the one with the door carved into
its trunk—was still there, but now, the verse beneath it had
changed.

"In the hollow heart of the tree,
    The Seeker waits, both blind and free.
    Enter the door; the price you'll pay,
    Will bind you here, or cast you away."

A shiver ran through Evan as the words sank in. He had been
drawn into this place—this world inside the poem—and it was
no longer a matter of curiosity. There were rules here. He didn't
understand them, but he could feel them pressing in on him
like an invisible weight.

Something moved in the mist, and he spun toward it, heart
hammering in his chest. At first, there was nothing, but then, a

figure emerged from the fog.

A woman. Tall, draped in a flowing cloak of midnight blue that shimmered faintly in the mist. Her face was obscured by a veil of silver threads, but her eyes—dark and knowing—pierced through the strands.

She stopped a few feet from him, her gaze unwavering.

"You're here," she said, her voice a soft, melodic whisper that seemed to echo from all around him.

"Where am I?" Evan repeated, his voice rough.

"The Seeker's Realm," she answered simply, as though it were the most obvious thing in the world. "You've crossed over. And now, you must choose."

"Choose?" Evan's breath quickened, his heart thudding in his chest. He looked around, panic creeping in. "I didn't ask for this. I just... I need to get back."

The woman's lips curled into something that might have been a smile, but it didn't reach her eyes. "You cannot go back."

The words hit him like a physical blow. "What do you mean I can't go back?" His voice cracked, the edges of his fear bleeding through.

"You've stepped beyond the veil," she said, as if that explained everything. "The manuscript brought you here. Now, it will be your guide—or your judge."

Evan took a step back, his mind reeling. "I didn't want this! I didn't want to be part of whatever this is!"

The woman raised a hand, her fingers delicate and long. "The poem is already a part of you. You are bound to it now."

A sudden gust of wind whipped through the trees, sending the mist swirling in every direction. The woman didn't flinch, but Evan staggered back, clutching the manuscript tightly to his chest. The wind carried with it a whisper—a voice so faint that he almost couldn't hear it, but it was unmistakable.

"Find the Seeker's Door."

It was the same phrase from the page.

"Who... Who is the Seeker?" Evan asked, his throat dry.

"The Seeker is the keeper of all the stories," she said, her voice growing colder. "The one who watches over those who are lost in the poem. The one who decides who stays, and who fades into nothing."

Evan's mind raced. "I don't want to fade into nothing. I just... I want to leave. I want to go home."

The woman's eyes softened for a moment, and she nodded. "The Seeker's Door is your only way out."

Evan's eyes darted to the distant trees, the image of the door carved into the trunk flashing in his mind. "Where is it?"

"You must find it yourself."

He shook his head, frustration bubbling to the surface. "How? I have no idea where to start!"

She studied him for a long moment, then took a step toward him. When she spoke again, her voice dropped, low and almost intimate. "The poem will guide you. But beware, Evan. The words are not always kind to those who seek too eagerly."

The wind picked up again, and the forest seemed to shift around him, the shadows lengthening, the air thick with unseen forces. For a moment, Evan could have sworn he saw something moving just beyond the trees—dark shapes, shifting and twitching like they were watching him.

"Stay on the path," the woman said, as if reading his thoughts. "And don't let the whispers lead you astray."

Without another word, she turned and began to walk away, her form dissolving into the mist like a ghost.

Evan stood there for a long time, the weight of her words pressing down on him. The forest seemed to close in, the shadows deeper now, and the whispering voices more distinct. He felt the manuscript pulse in his hands again, as though it were urging him forward.

The trees ahead of him parted, and in the distance, he saw it—a great oak, its bark darkened with age, a door carved into its trunk. The door was old, weathered, and just barely visible in the half-light, as though it had been waiting for him.

Evan stepped toward it, his feet unsteady, but his resolve hardening. The whispers grew louder, swirling around him in a frenzy, but he couldn't make out the words. Only one thing was clear: the door was the way out. He had to enter.

As his hand reached for the handle, he heard the voice again—the woman's voice, distant but clear.

"Remember, Evan... the poem never lets go."

With a final breath, he pushed the door open.

5

The Price of Passage

The door creaked open with a groan that echoed like a warning. The world beyond was dim, an expanse of foggy nothingness. It felt like stepping into a void, as if the very air was a liquid, thick and hard to move through. Evan hesitated at the threshold, the manuscript clutched tightly in his hands. Every instinct screamed at him to turn back, to run, to forget this madness and return to the world he knew. But the pull of the poem, of the place he was now trapped in, was stronger than any fear.

Behind him, the forest whispered. The wind rustled the branches, carrying with it something more than just the rustling of leaves. It was a hum—a low, vibrating sound that seemed to crawl under his skin, igniting every nerve with an overwhelming sense of urgency.

Without another glance back, Evan stepped through the door.

The moment his foot crossed the threshold, the world shifted violently.

The fog dissolved, and the air became cold, a biting chill that froze his breath in the air. He stood now in a cavernous, dimly lit hall. The walls were lined with shelves upon shelves of books— dozens of volumes, their spines cracked and aged, titles in languages Evan couldn't comprehend. The ceiling stretched high above him, disappearing into darkness. Strange, jagged shadows clung to the edges of the room like the remnants of forgotten memories. The only light came from an eerie glow that seemed to emanate from the books themselves, casting the room in an ethereal, greenish hue.

"Welcome," a voice said, so sudden and sharp that Evan jumped. He spun toward the sound, but no one was there. The voice was neither male nor female, but ancient, as though it had existed for longer than time itself.

"Who's there?" Evan demanded, his heart hammering against his chest.

The voice didn't respond immediately. Instead, it echoed, swirling around him, as if the very room itself were alive and listening. The books on the shelves rustled—pages turning, whispers seeping from their bindings. He took an involuntary step back, looking for an escape that wasn't there.

"The price of passage is always paid," the voice said finally, as if toying with him. "But not all who enter are prepared."

Evan clenched the manuscript in his hand, his fingers tight with anxiety. "What do you mean by 'price'?" His voice faltered, but he forced himself to stand tall. "I just want to get out of here. I need to leave."

The greenish light intensified, flickering like a heartbeat. The air grew heavier, thicker. The shadows began to shift again, but this time they seemed to form shapes—tall, indistinct figures, their outlines rippling like ink spilled into water.

"Leave?" The voice sounded almost amused. "The poem has claimed you. There is no leaving without a sacrifice."

Evan took a step backward, his mind racing. He glanced around, but all he could see were the shadows and the endless bookshelves, the twisting figures moving just out of his line of sight. He wasn't alone. He never had been. The feeling of being watched pressed against him, suffocating, maddening.

"What kind of sacrifice?" he demanded. "I never asked for any of this! I just—"

"You sought the truth," the voice interrupted, cold and unyielding. "And in doing so, you have agreed to the terms."

The shadows converged, drawing closer, and Evan's pulse quickened. He had to get answers. There had to be a way out, a way to end this nightmare before it consumed him entirely.

"Why me?" he whispered, his voice trembling. "Why did the poem choose me?"

"The poem does not choose," the voice responded. "It calls. And those who answer become part of it."

Suddenly, the shelves in front of him shifted, and a book slid from one of the upper shelves, falling to the ground with a thud. The pages fluttered open, and words began to scrawl themselves onto the pages, fresh ink appearing as if written by an invisible hand. Evan's breath caught in his throat as he recognized the writing—his own name.

The manuscript in his hands began to vibrate, humming in response. The ink on its pages shimmered, forming letters, then words. The verse he had seen earlier in the forest seemed to come alive, curling across the paper in elegant strokes. But this time, the words were different—dark, ominous.

"The Seeker waits beyond the veil,
   In a place where no light prevails.
   The price you pay is steep and true,
   A part of you shall stay, not you."

Evan's stomach churned, nausea rising. The words had changed, warped into something sinister, and he felt as though the manuscript was devouring him, its ink sinking into his skin, into his very soul.

The shadows around him thickened. They were no longer abstract shapes—they were figures now, tangible, reaching toward him with cold, grasping hands. He stumbled back, his heart racing in panic, but they were faster. One of the figures lunged at him, its hand wrapping around his wrist with an icy grip.

"You cannot escape the poem," the voice whispered, now

surrounding him, filling his head, his heart. "Not unless you give it what it desires."

"NO!" Evan cried, wrenching his arm free with all his strength. "I'm not giving you anything! I want out!"

But the figure's grip tightened, and suddenly, the shadows began to pull him forward, dragging him closer to the shelves. The books rattled and shifted, the words on the pages blurring and warping, as though the very library was alive and trying to swallow him whole.

Evan twisted and struggled, but the shadows were relentless. He could feel his energy draining, the world around him spinning, the manuscript still clutched in his hands, its pages now turning on their own.

The voice laughed softly, like the rustle of dry leaves. "You will pay the price, Evan. You will stay, or you will fade away."

Just when it seemed like the shadows would consume him entirely, a loud crash rang through the room. The shelves trembled, and the shadows recoiled, momentarily releasing their grip on him. The source of the disturbance came from above. Evan's eyes shot to the ceiling, but before he could react, something descended from the darkness—a figure, large and imposing, cloaked in black, its face obscured by a hood.

The figure moved with unsettling speed, its hands outstretched toward Evan, but the shadows retreated in its wake. There was something about the figure that repelled them, something that made the very air shift in its presence.

"Enough," the figure's voice rumbled, deep and powerful. "The boy is mine."

Evan didn't know whether to feel relief or more dread. Was this another part of the poem? Another price to pay?

"Who are you?" he gasped, his breath shallow.

The figure didn't answer right away. Instead, it reached out and touched the manuscript in Evan's hands, its fingers brushing lightly over the pages. The book seemed to tremble in response, the ink swirling beneath the hooded figure's touch. The figure spoke again, its voice a low growl.

"You've entered the story, boy. Now you must finish it."

Before Evan could ask what that meant, the figure pulled him forward, toward the shelf that had opened in front of him. The pages in the manuscript began to turn faster, as though they had a mind of their own. The whispers grew louder, each word sharper than the last, each one more insistent.

"Finish it. Finish it. Finish it..."

And then, without warning, the shadows closed in again, the figure's grip tightening on Evan's wrist, pulling him deeper into the darkness. The price was about to be paid.

6

The Hollow Echo

Evan's mind swam in a fog of disorientation as the figure's grip tightened, pulling him deeper into the darkness. His heart raced, panic flooding his veins. The shadows that had once been mere shapes now felt like a tangible force, wrapping around him, suffocating him with an oppressive weight. The manuscript in his hands flickered with light as if trying to burn through his skin, the ink twisting and coiling as the pages turned on their own accord, each movement mocking his desperation.

"Where are you taking me?" he gasped, struggling to break free. But the figure—tall, imposing, with a hood that seemed to consume the very light—pulled him further into the cavernous room, its silence deafening.

There was no escape. He could feel it. The walls seemed to stretch endlessly, closing in on him, and the floor beneath his feet felt soft, almost sponge-like, as though it were shifting with every step, threatening to swallow him whole. The strange, cold air carried a scent that was both foul and sweet, like decaying flowers.

"You are not the first to walk this path," the figure said, its voice low, almost reverberating through the air. It was as if the words were not just heard, but felt—deep within his bones. "And you will not be the last. The poem claims all who enter."

Evan wanted to scream. He wanted to throw the manuscript away, to rip it apart, to escape whatever this was. But his hands were frozen to it, as if the very act of letting go would tear him apart from the inside out. The whispers in his mind grew louder, echoing through his skull, all of them murmuring the same thing.

"Finish it. Finish it."

"I can't," Evan muttered under his breath, his voice barely a whisper. "I don't even know what it wants from me."

The figure stopped, its shadow stretching across the room like a living thing. It slowly turned toward him, and Evan felt a cold shiver crawl up his spine as its hooded face loomed closer. When it spoke again, the voice was almost a whisper—a cold, hollow sound that seemed to come from all around him.

"You must give something of yourself," it said, its tone unyielding. "A part of your soul, a fragment of your being. Only then will the path be cleared, and the way forward revealed."

Evan recoiled, the grip on the manuscript tightening. "No... I won't give you anything. I just want to leave!"

The figure was silent for a long moment. Then, with a slow, deliberate motion, it lifted its hand, a finger pointing directly at Evan. The air around him grew even colder, and the shadows seemed to pulse, drawing closer, closing in on him.

"You are already part of the story," the figure said, its voice like a dark lullaby. "And the story will never let you go."

Suddenly, the world around him seemed to shift once more, the shelves and books around them dissolving into thin air. The room was no longer a cavernous hall but a vast, endless void. A hollow echo reverberated through the emptiness, as if the very space they occupied was a mere reflection of something deeper—something darker. Evan could hear nothing but the faint, almost imperceptible whispers, growing louder and louder.

"Do you hear them?" the figure asked, its voice now a distant, distant hum. "The echoes of those who have been claimed before you. The ones who never left."

Evan's breath quickened. He could hear it now, a steady rhythm—like the ticking of a clock, but slower, heavier, filled with a sense of dread. It was an oppressive sound that filled the emptiness of the space, drawing him closer to the edge of madness.

"You will not leave, Evan," the figure continued. "Not without paying the price. Not without becoming a part of it. The story will not be finished until it takes what it wants from you."

The words sent a jolt through Evan's chest, his heart racing. He couldn't breathe, couldn't think. The manuscript was too heavy in his hands now, its pages turning faster, its ink bleeding into his skin. The words began to warp again, the lines of the poem twisting into something unrecognizable, each line pulling him deeper into the narrative, into the poem itself.

"Stop it!" Evan shouted, feeling a surge of desperate energy. "I won't give you anything!"

But the shadows only closed in tighter, surrounding him, tightening their grip. The hollow echo reverberated louder, and the words on the pages now bled together in a chaos of ink and madness. Evan screamed, but no sound left his mouth. His vision blurred, and the darkness seemed to stretch out forever, swallowing him whole.

And then, as if the very fabric of reality was being torn apart, there was a sudden shift. A break in the darkness. The room around him split open, and a blinding light flooded the space, pushing back the shadows.

For a moment, Evan thought he was free. But the light didn't feel like salvation—it felt like something else. Like it was waiting, watching. It was as if the light had always been there, lurking just beyond the shadows, waiting to claim him.

He didn't have time to react before something—a presence— emerged from the light. It was a figure, tall and thin, with sharp features that seemed to shimmer in the light, like a reflection of something he could barely comprehend. It moved with grace, with purpose, its movements fluid and almost predatory.

And then the voice came again—the voice that had haunted him from the very beginning. The same voice that had whispered to him in the forest, in the cavern, in the darkness.

"You have made your choice," the voice said softly, its tone impossibly calm, despite the chaos swirling around them. "Now, you must face what you have unleashed."

The figure in the light moved closer to him, its eyes—bright, piercing, and utterly unyielding—fixed on his. The light pulsed with energy, and Evan felt his chest tighten as if the very air around him had become solid, pressing in from all sides.

"I didn't choose this!" he cried, his voice cracking. "I didn't ask for any of this!"

The figure's lips curved into a thin smile, but it was not comforting—it was something darker, something that promised the inevitable.

"The poem chooses those who seek it," the figure said, its voice now clear, sharp, and final. "And once you have entered, there is no way out. You will give it what it wants, whether you choose to or not."

Evan's knees buckled, his body trembling with a fear so over-whelming he could barely stand. The manuscript's presence was suffocating now, the pages still turning on their own, the words now a blur of ink and madness.

But the figure did not reach for him. Instead, it raised a hand, and with a single motion, a portal opened before him—a door that had not been there a moment ago, a swirling vortex of darkness and light.

"Enter," the figure commanded, its voice echoing in the space around him. "And finish the story, Evan. If you do not, you will be lost to it forever."

For a long moment, Evan stood frozen, his mind racing, his heart pounding in his chest. The words on the manuscript screamed at him, urging him toward the portal. The whispers intensified, their voices now a chorus, beckoning him forward.

With no other choice, no other hope of escape, Evan took a deep breath and stepped toward the door. The light from the figure flickered, casting long shadows as the portal opened wider, ready to swallow him whole.

And as he crossed the threshold, the hollow echo of the poem's call seemed to consume everything, leaving him with nothing but the empty promise of what was to come.

7

The Heart of Silence

The moment Evan stepped through the portal, the world shifted in a violent, disorienting rush. The air around him thickened, becoming dense and cold. He gasped for breath, but it felt as though he were drowning in the very atmosphere. His body felt heavy, weighted down by something invisible, like an unseen force pressing against him from all sides. The manuscript in his hands trembled, as though it, too, was affected by the pressure of this new place, and its pages fluttered urgently, as though it were alive.

When the pressure lifted, Evan opened his eyes. The landscape before him was like nothing he had ever seen. It wasn't a place he could have imagined, nor one he could have ever understood. It was a barren, desolate wasteland, an endless expanse of cracked earth that stretched far beyond the horizon. The sky above was a swirling, unnatural shade of gray—neither stormy nor clear, but a color that seemed to vibrate with tension, like a bruise that refused to fade. The ground was jagged, the jagged stones jutting out of the earth at odd angles, as if something deep below had torn through the surface, and the land had never quite healed.

But it wasn't the landscape that made Evan's heart race. It was the silence.

It was a silence so profound, so absolute, that it felt like the world was holding its breath, waiting. Every step Evan took seemed to be swallowed by it. The only sound was the faint crackle of the manuscript in his hands, the whisper of its pages turning as the ink shifted beneath his fingertips. The air was so still, so thick, that even his own heartbeat felt muffled, as though the rhythm of his life had been muted in this strange place.

The absence of sound was almost worse than any noise he had ever heard. It was a vacuum, an emptiness that gnawed at him, pulling at his sanity. In the distance, towering black structures rose from the earth, their edges sharp and angular, casting long, jagged shadows across the wasteland. They seemed to watch him, cold and silent, like the eyes of a forgotten god.

He stumbled forward, his legs unsteady as though the ground beneath him was unstable, shifting with every step. The manuscript's weight in his hands grew heavier, its presence an unrelenting reminder that this was not just a place he had entered, but a place he was part of now. The words on the pages burned beneath his fingers, insistent, relentless.

The whispers began again, quieter this time, but still persistent.

"You're here to finish it, Evan. You're here to finish what you started."

A gust of wind stirred the barren landscape, but even it seemed muffled, like a distant memory. The ground under his feet shifted slightly, and for a moment, the silence was shattered by the faintest sound—a low, grinding, metallic noise.

Evan froze, his heart slamming in his chest as his eyes darted around the desolation, searching for the source. There was nothing, only the oppressive silence and the weight of the manuscript in his hands. But the noise came again, closer this time, followed by the faintest echo of something heavy dragging across the earth.

His pulse quickened. His mind screamed at him to run, but his legs refused to move. The sound grew louder, closer, and suddenly, a shape appeared in the distance. A dark, hulking figure, moving slowly across the cracked earth. It was impossibly tall, its form distorted, its edges shifting and blurring like smoke. As it drew nearer, the noise grew louder—a rasping, dragging sound as if the creature's very body scraped across the ground, leaving trails of blackened earth in its wake.

Evan took a step back, his breath quickening. The figure loomed closer, its shape solidifying. Its body was a mass of shadow and darkness, but there was something disturbingly human about it. Its limbs were long, grotesquely elongated, its hands reaching out with fingers too long to be real. Its face—if it could be called a face—was a blank slate, an empty void where eyes should have been. A gaping mouth opened wide, revealing rows of sharp teeth that gleamed in the strange light, though there was no sound. Only that heavy dragging noise, filling the silence like a scream without a voice.

Evan stumbled backward, the manuscript slipping from his hands as he tried to run, but his legs felt like lead. His movements were sluggish, as if the very air were weighing him down. The creature's presence filled the space around him, making it feel smaller, more suffocating.

He turned to look for an escape, but the landscape had changed. The towering black structures had moved, shifting in the distance like monolithic shadows. There was no safe place, no hiding spot. He was trapped.

The creature's head turned toward him, its empty gaze settling on him with a predatory intent. For a moment, the world seemed to stop. The silence deepened, becoming suffocating, and Evan's throat closed up, his breathing shallow. He couldn't move. He couldn't speak. He was rooted to the spot, paralyzed by the weight of its gaze, by the sense that this creature had always been here, waiting for him.

Then, without warning, the creature lunged forward, its long limbs stretching unnaturally as it closed the distance between them in a single, swift motion. Evan barely had time to react before it was upon him, its shadowy form enveloping him, its cold, unfeeling presence pressing in from all sides.

He screamed, a raw, primal cry, but the sound was swallowed by the silence before it could even escape his lips. The creature's cold hands grasped him with a strength that made his bones crack, lifting him off the ground with ease. He kicked and thrashed, but it was as though his body were weightless, as though he were a puppet being controlled by invisible strings. The creature's form flickered, blurring and distorting, but its grip never loosened.

Evan's vision swam, the edges of his mind fraying, as the creature dragged him through the desolation, toward the towering black structures. The whispers in his head grew louder, more insistent, until they were a cacophony, all of them speaking at once, urging him to finish the poem, to give in, to submit.

And then, with a sudden, horrifying clarity, Evan understood. This was the heart of the poem—the place where it was born, where it had always been. This was where the darkness lived, where the story had been waiting for him. The creatures, the shadows, the silence—it was all part of the poem, all part of the price he had to pay. The story had claimed him, and now it would devour him.

The creature lifted him higher, its dark face drawing closer, the void of its eyes now a bottomless abyss. As it opened its mouth, Evan could feel the cold, suffocating air rushing toward him, the void pulling him in, ready to swallow him whole.

But just as he thought he would be consumed by it, there was a sudden flash of light—a brilliant, blinding burst that tore through the darkness. The creature recoiled, its grip loosening as it shrieked, a sound that was pure agony, though no sound escaped its lips. The world around Evan rippled, shifting, as the manuscript in his hands flared to life, its pages glowing with an intense light.

The silence was broken—not by noise, but by the weight of the words themselves. The manuscript was alive, and the story was shifting again, pulling him deeper into the darkness. Evan's eyes blurred as the words on the page began to form something new, something terrible.

He had no choice but to read.

And as he did, the ground beneath him trembled, and the sky above began to fracture. The price had been paid. The heart of the poem had been unlocked, and now there was no turning back.

8

The Echoing Void

Evan's hands trembled as he clutched the manuscript, its pages glowing with an eerie, unnatural light. His breath came in short, shallow gasps as the world around him pulsed with a rhythm that was not his own. He felt as if the ground beneath him was alive, breathing, shifting in sync with the pounding of his heart. The towering black structures loomed even larger now, their shadows stretching across the land like long fingers, reaching for him.

The creature—whatever it had been—was gone. But in its place, a suffocating silence hung in the air, thick and heavy, almost tangible. The air itself seemed to crackle with an unseen energy, as though the very fabric of reality was being torn apart. The manuscript's glow grew brighter, its words becoming sharper, clearer, the ink on the pages swirling as though it were alive.

But Evan couldn't bring himself to turn the pages anymore. The words, now etched in his mind, burned in his thoughts like a fever, their weight crushing him with every breath. Finish it.

Complete the story. The voice in his head had become one with the words, a constant, unyielding presence.

The ground shook again, a low, rumbling tremor that reverberated through the earth. The structures in the distance began to shift, their jagged forms twisting and contorting as if they were being molded by an unseen force. Evan's mind raced, panic clawing at the edges of his thoughts. Where was he? What was this place? The silence had become a living thing, its presence pressing in on him from all sides, suffocating him, making him feel small, insignificant.

The air felt wrong, like it was pressing against him, making it harder to breathe. He stumbled, his feet unsteady, his mind unhinged by the oppressive weight of the silence. And then he saw it.

A figure in the distance. Small at first, but growing larger with every passing second. It moved unnaturally fast, its silhouette jagged, its limbs stretching out in ways that defied logic. It was humanoid in shape, but its proportions were distorted, exaggerated, almost grotesque. The more Evan stared, the more it seemed to flicker, shifting like a glitch in reality.

His heart skipped a beat. The figure was coming closer.

Desperately, Evan tried to take a step back, but his legs felt like lead, as though they were no longer under his control. His mind screamed at him to run, to escape, but the words of the poem echoed louder, pulling him forward. Finish it. Complete the story. The voice was not his own. It was coming from the manuscript, from the world around him, from the very space he occupied.

The figure was now only a few feet away, its unnatural movement like the flapping of some great, monstrous bird, its limbs jerking in an erratic dance. It paused, its head tilting as though it were studying him, its blank, featureless face frozen in a silent scream. And then, in the stillness, it spoke.

"You think you can escape?" The voice was cold, flat, like a whisper in a tomb. "You're part of it now. The story claims you, just as it claimed all the others."

Evan's breath caught in his throat. His pulse hammered in his ears as the figure stepped forward, its presence consuming him, the silence around them so thick he could feel it pressing against his chest. The glow from the manuscript seemed to pulse in rhythm with his heartbeat, each thud of his pulse making the world around him distort even more, like the ground was shifting, bending in response to his fear.

"I—I don't want this!" Evan shouted, his voice barely a whisper against the silence. He raised the manuscript in front of him as though it could protect him, but the words blurred, the ink swirling like smoke, unreadable and incomprehensible.

The figure didn't move, didn't react. It just stared at him, its gaze piercing, unyielding. The longer Evan looked, the more he felt himself drawn into it, as if the very air between them was a web, a trap that he could never escape from.

"You never had a choice," the figure continued, its voice now an eerie, melodic hum that seemed to vibrate through Evan's bones. "The poem chose you, just as it has chosen countless others. It doesn't matter what you want. It never has."

The words settled into Evan's mind, filling every crevice, every thought. The silence grew heavier, more oppressive, until it felt like the very walls of his mind were closing in. His breath became shallow, his chest tight with the weight of it all. And yet, despite the panic threatening to drown him, there was a strange pull, a lure, as though the poem was calling to him, urging him to finish it.

"Do you hear it?" the figure asked, its voice now a breath, barely audible. "The echo of those who came before you? The ones who couldn't finish? They're all here, waiting. You're not the first to be claimed."

Evan's eyes widened. The air around him seemed to thrum with an energy he couldn't explain. It was as though the very space between him and the figure was alive, vibrating with the energy of forgotten voices. From the edge of his vision, he saw them— shadows, faint and distant, flickering in and out of existence. Faces, blurred and indistinct, filled the air around him. They whispered, their voices a chorus of desperation, begging for release.

The manuscript in his hands shook violently, the pages flipping rapidly, faster than he could comprehend. The words on the page began to form again, this time clearer, darker, their meaning unmistakable.

The poem was never finished. It was waiting for you. And once you've completed it, there is no return.

A sickening realization bloomed in his chest, a cold, twisting feeling that had nothing to do with the terror gnawing at his insides. He was not just part of the story—he was its end. The poem had been unfinished, incomplete, and now, as he stood on the precipice of whatever this place was, the final lines were waiting for him to write them. And once he did, there would be no going back. No escape.

"No," Evan gasped, his voice cracking. He looked around, desperately searching for any sign of salvation, but the darkness, the silence, and the figures were closing in. The shapes in the distance moved toward him, their twisted forms growing clearer as they approached. They were the faces of those who had failed, those who had been consumed by the poem before him.

"Don't do it," the figure whispered, its voice now a lullaby, soothing, almost kind. "It's already too late."

The last flicker of hope that had remained in Evan's chest withered and died as the manuscript grew hotter in his hands. The pages burned, the words demanding to be read, to be finished. The whispers grew louder, the figures surrounding him now fully formed, their hollow eyes staring at him with silent accusation.

And then, as if the world were folding in on itself, a single, final line appeared on the manuscript.

The heart of silence must be broken.

Evan's breath caught in his throat. The words were simple, yet they carried an unbearable weight. The silence that had once been oppressive now felt like a wound, a wound that could only be healed by finishing what had been started.

As he read the words aloud, the silence shattered with a deafening crack. The world around him trembled, and the shadows reached out, pulling him in. The figures whispered, their voices now a cacophony of torment, their hands grasping at him, pulling him deeper into the void.

And as the world fell away, Evan understood—he had become part of the poem, just as it had become part of him. The story had claimed him, and now it was finished.

9

The Face of the Writer

The world around Evan was shifting again. The blackened sky, once a swirling abyss of gray, had begun to take on a more vibrant hue—an unsettling shade of red that seemed to pulse with every beat of his heart. The earth beneath him still trembled, but now, it had a rhythm, like the world itself was breathing. Each breath, slow and deliberate, made him feel more and more as though he were not walking through reality, but rather, moving through some grotesque, half-formed dream.

The faces, those hollow, distorted faces, were gone now, absorbed by the shadows that still lingered at the edges of his vision. The whispers, too, had quieted—replaced by an eerie silence that felt even more suffocating than the one before. He could feel the manuscript in his hands growing heavier, its presence growing more insistent with each passing second. The ink on its pages had stopped moving, the words now static and fixed in place, as though they had finally solidified, settled into their final form. But the weight of the story still pressed upon him, like an invisible hand tightening around his chest.

Evan stumbled, his feet dragging through the barren landscape. He had no sense of direction, no sense of time. The world around him seemed to stretch on forever, a barren wasteland with no end in sight. And yet, he couldn't shake the feeling that he was being watched—monitored by something that existed just beyond his reach.

A sudden flash of movement caught his eye, and he spun toward it. There, in the distance, a figure stood. At first, it seemed to be little more than a shadow, a dark shape against the backdrop of the red sky. But as it drew closer, Evan's heart clenched with a jolt of recognition.

It was a man, tall and lean, with sharp features that seemed to shimmer in and out of existence. His face was half-obscured by a wide-brimmed hat, but there was no mistaking the glint of cold, calculating eyes that peered from beneath the shadow of his hat. The figure moved with an eerie grace, his footsteps leaving no mark on the ground, as though he were walking on air.

Evan froze. The man's presence was somehow both familiar and foreign, as though he were someone Evan should know, but couldn't quite place. The sense of recognition gnawed at him, digging into the corners of his mind, pulling at memories he couldn't quite recall.

As the man drew closer, Evan's pulse quickened. There was something undeniably sinister about him. The way he moved, the way he seemed to bend the very air around him—it was as though he didn't belong in this world at all. He was part of something darker, something that Evan couldn't yet understand.

"You've been looking for me," the man said, his voice a low, gravelly whisper that seemed to echo through the silence. The words sent a chill down Evan's spine. "I'm the one you've been chasing all this time."

Evan's mouth went dry. He opened his mouth to speak, but no words came. His thoughts were a jumbled mess, swirling in a vortex of confusion. This man—this figure—had to be a part of the story. But how? Was he the writer? Was he the one who had created this nightmare?

The man took a step closer, and Evan felt the air grow colder. The heat of the red sky was nothing compared to the cold emanating from the figure before him. It was a bone-deep chill that crept into his very soul, making his teeth chatter despite the sweat that slicked his skin.

"Do you know who I am?" the man asked, his tone almost amused, as though Evan's confusion entertained him. "Do you know why you're here?"

Evan swallowed, struggling to find his voice. The man's eyes bore into him, and he felt as though the weight of his gaze was pulling him deeper into the world that surrounded him—into the story itself.

"I... I don't understand," Evan muttered, his voice shaky. "Who are you?"

The man smiled, the expression cold and knowing. He reached up, removing his hat with a slow, deliberate motion. As the brim lifted, Evan's breath caught in his throat.

The man's face was nothing like what Evan had expected. It was not just the sharp features or the hollow eyes that unnerved him—it was the fact that the man's face seemed... familiar. Too familiar. It was a reflection of Evan himself.

Evan staggered backward, his heart hammering in his chest. This was impossible. This couldn't be happening. His eyes darted from the man's face to his own hands, as though expecting some kind of change, some proof that this was all a nightmare. But everything was the same. The world around him was the same. He was trapped in a place where the rules didn't apply, where the boundaries of reality had long since collapsed.

The man, or rather, the thing that looked like him, took another step forward. "It's not just the poem that brings you here," he said, his voice now an eerie echo of Evan's own thoughts. "It's you. You're the key. You're the one who's been writing this story all along."

Evan's mind reeled. Writing the story? How could that be? He hadn't written this, hadn't even known it existed until it had consumed him. The words on the pages of the manuscript were not his—they were someone else's, someone who had written them long before he had ever come across them. Weren't they?

The man's smile widened. "The poem needs you, Evan. You think it's some distant creation, some piece of fiction, but you're wrong. It's part of you. It's always been part of you."

"No," Evan whispered, shaking his head, his breath coming in short, panicked bursts. "I didn't—this isn't my story. I'm not—"

The man's hand shot out, gripping Evan's arm with a force that made him gasp. His grip was cold, impossibly cold, and as Evan looked down, he saw that the man's fingers were not flesh, but blackened, cracked stone. The veins in his hand were like twisted roots, as though the man's body was made of the very earth beneath them.

"It's always been yours," the man repeated, his voice now a growl, a low rumble that reverberated through Evan's bones. "You were born to write it. To finish it. You're not just a character, Evan. You're the creator."

Evan's mind struggled to grasp the meaning of the words. He had to be wrong. This wasn't possible. He wasn't the creator. He was the one trapped inside it. He was the one who had been pulled into this story. And yet, the longer he stared at the man, the more he felt the truth seep into his bones.

The man laughed, a sound that was both a warning and a revelation. "You're part of it, Evan. Part of the story. And whether you like it or not, you will finish it."

Before Evan could react, the man's eyes flashed with an intense, searing light, and the world around him began to crumble. The ground cracked beneath his feet, the sky above splintering like glass, sending shards of red light scattering into the air. The man's form began to dissolve, as if he were being consumed by the very words of the poem.

And then, as quickly as it had started, the world went silent again. Evan was left standing alone, the manuscript still gripped tightly in his hands. His heart pounded in his chest as the realization struck him with brutal force.

He wasn't just trapped in the story. He was the story. And now, there was no turning back.

10

The Hollow Archive

Evan stood at the edge of the cliff, his breath shallow, his heart racing as he stared out over the vast expanse below. There was no sound, no movement, just the oppressive silence pressing in from all directions. The red sky stretched endlessly, its blood-red hue growing deeper with each passing second. It was as though the world itself had become a wound that had never healed, the air thick with the scent of decay.

His fingers tightened around the manuscript, now burning hot against his skin. The words on the pages had become more and more legible, clearer than ever before, but they made no sense. They twisted and turned like an endless loop, a spiral that had no end. He could feel them tugging at the edges of his mind, urging him to follow them, to complete the final chapter.

But he didn't want to. The very thought of finishing it made him recoil. There was something in those final words—a dark, dangerous promise—that made his blood run cold. Yet, the pull was undeniable. It was as if the story had taken root inside him, its tendrils wrapping around his soul, and now, there was no escaping it.

With a sharp exhale, he turned away from the edge, trying to shake off the suffocating feeling that clung to him. The ground beneath his feet shifted, and suddenly, the landscape around him began to change. The barren wasteland morphed, the air growing dense with the smell of paper and ink, the very scent of a library. But this wasn't any ordinary library—it was something darker, something older, something that had never been meant to exist.

Evan blinked, and when he opened his eyes again, he found himself standing in front of an enormous door, made of what appeared to be worn leather and bound with thick, iron clasps. The door loomed before him like an impenetrable fortress, its surface etched with symbols that seemed to shimmer in the low light. His hand hesitated for a moment before he reached for the handle, the cold metal biting into his palm as he gripped it.

The door creaked open with a sound that echoed through the vast emptiness around him. As it swung wide, a dark, cavernous room unfolded before him, stretching farther than he could see. The shelves were stacked high with rows upon rows of dusty, forgotten books, their spines cracked and faded with age. The air was thick with the weight of knowledge—ancient, untold knowledge—and it pressed down on him, suffocating him with its oppressive presence.

But something was wrong.

As Evan stepped inside, the shadows seemed to move. They twisted and writhed, shifting in the corner of his vision, just beyond his reach. The silence that filled the room was deafening, the kind of silence that makes your thoughts feel like an intruder. He couldn't shake the feeling that something—someone—was watching him from the darkness.

With a flicker of uncertainty, he took a step forward, his footsteps muffled by the thick carpet of dust beneath him. He couldn't explain it, but there was something familiar about this place. It was as if he had been here before, long ago, in another life. The realization sent a shiver down his spine, and his hand instinctively tightened around the manuscript.

The shelves seemed to stretch on forever, their contents un-reachable, as though the books themselves were locked away in another world. But there, in the distance, was something different. Something... alive. Evan's gaze shifted, drawn to a small table in the center of the room. Atop it lay an open book, its pages filled with words he could not decipher, its language ancient and twisted.

A chill ran down his spine, and without thinking, he moved toward the table. As his hand reached for the book, a voice— soft, barely audible—echoed through the room.

"You shouldn't open that."

Evan froze, his heart stuttering in his chest. The voice had come from behind him. Slowly, he turned, his eyes scanning the shadows, but there was no one there.

Another voice, louder this time, pierced the silence. "You're too late."

Evan's pulse quickened. There was something in the room—something alive, something watching him from the darkness. He could feel its presence, a weight pressing in from every corner, its eyes unseen but undeniably real.

"Who's there?" he demanded, his voice trembling. The words felt wrong in the heavy silence, swallowed by the darkness that surrounded him.

For a long moment, there was no answer. The only sound was the soft rustle of pages turning, as though the very air was shifting with the turning of a book. Evan's mind raced, his thoughts a blur. He couldn't stay here. He had to get out.

But as he turned toward the door, a shadow moved at the edge of his vision, and he froze.

It was a figure—tall, thin, with long, spindly limbs that seemed to stretch unnaturally. It stood in the doorway, its face hidden in the folds of its dark cloak. The figure didn't move, didn't speak. It simply watched.

Evan's breath hitched. He knew this figure. He couldn't explain how, but he recognized it. The same way he had recognized the man with the hat earlier. The feeling of familiarity, of something twisted and wrong, settled deep in his gut.

"You shouldn't have come here," the figure said, its voice a rasping whisper, like dry paper tearing. "The library is not for you."

Evan took a step back, his mind screaming for him to run, to escape this place, but his feet were frozen in place. The figure raised a hand, the fingers long and skeletal, and pointed toward the book on the table.

"Open it, if you must," it said, its voice growing colder, more menacing. "But know that once you do, there is no turning back. The story has already begun. And you, Evan, are its final chapter."

The words echoed in Evan's mind like a death knell. His gaze shifted toward the book, the one lying innocently on the table, its pages waiting to be turned. The urge to open it was overwhelming, a compulsion that he could no longer fight. It was the same pull, the same dark lure that had led him here, that had driven him to the edge of insanity.

But the figure's words gnawed at him. There is no turning back.

He was trapped in the story. And every step he took, every decision he made, only deepened his entanglement in its twisted, unrelenting narrative.

With shaking hands, Evan reached for the book. The moment his fingers brushed the pages, a violent tremor coursed through his body, and the room seemed to ripple with energy. The shelves groaned, the air thick with the weight of ancient knowledge, and the shadows that had once seemed distant and disconnected now rushed forward, enveloping him.

The figure in the doorway stepped forward, its face finally emerging from the shadows. And as Evan looked into its eyes, he saw—himself.

The world around him shattered, the boundaries between reality and fiction dissolving as the final words of the manuscript called out to him, pulling him deeper into the dark heart of the story.

And Evan realized, with sickening clarity, that he had always been part of it. The hollow archive, the endless rows of forgotten books, the shadows that whispered in the dark—it was all him. Every word, every twist, every turn had been written by his own hand. And now, as the figure in the doorway smiled, he understood. The story would never end. Not for him. Not for anyone.

The final chapter had already been written.

11

The Writer's Dilemma

Evan's pulse pounded in his ears as he stood frozen, the manuscript still clutched tightly in his hands. The world around him had shifted, the weight of the library pressing in from all sides, suffocating him with its endless rows of books and pages of forgotten secrets. He could feel the air growing heavy with something—something ancient, something that shouldn't have been allowed to exist. The whispers, those faint, insidious murmurs, were back again, sliding beneath his skin, urging him to listen, to understand. But Evan wasn't sure he wanted to.

He wasn't sure he could understand.

His breath hitched as the figure—the one who had spoken, the one who had revealed himself to be a reflection of Evan— stepped forward. The air thickened with tension, and every step it took echoed like a drumbeat in the cavernous room, reverberating in his chest. The figure's face, now fully visible, was not just a mirror image of his own; it was a twisted, distorted version of him, as though the story had taken every piece of his identity and reshaped it into something darker, more grotesque.

The figure smiled, its lips stretching unnaturally wide, revealing teeth that seemed far too sharp for a human mouth. "You've been searching for answers," it said, its voice a soft, mocking cadence that made Evan's skin crawl. "But the only answer that matters is the one you refuse to face."

Evan stepped back, his hands trembling, but the manuscript felt as though it were glued to his palms, the pages still hot with an otherworldly energy. His mind raced, heart hammering. He had to get out of here. He had to wake up. None of this made sense. None of it. He had only been following the words, following the pull of the story, never once thinking that he might be creating it as much as he was living it. The realization was a heavy weight pressing down on him, suffocating him with its implications.

"Why?" Evan choked out, his voice trembling. "Why me? Why this story?"

The figure tilted its head, as though considering the question, its dark eyes glimmering with something that might have been pity—or amusement. "You think you have no part in this? That you are just a pawn in some grand design? No, Evan. You are the architect. The creator. The writer."

The word sent a shiver down Evan's spine. The writer. The architect of his own misery, his own demise. It wasn't just the story that was trapping him here; it was his own hand, his own mind, that had woven this nightmare into existence.

"You've always known," the figure continued, its voice low and hypnotic. "From the moment you picked up the manuscript, you knew that this was more than just a book. This was your prison. This was your legacy. Your destiny."

Evan felt the room close in on him, the shelves of ancient books pressing down like a weight, the air thick with the scent of decaying paper. It was as if the very walls were alive, breathing in time with the rhythm of his frantic heartbeat. The shadows seemed to shift and lengthen, growing darker with every passing second, until the corners of the room were consumed by an impenetrable blackness.

He took another step back, his legs unsteady beneath him. "No. I—I didn't mean for any of this to happen," he whispered, more to himself than to the figure. "This wasn't supposed to be real."

The figure's eyes gleamed with a cruel satisfaction. "It was never supposed to be real. But it is. And now, you must finish it."

The words hit Evan like a physical blow. Finish it. There it was again, that demand, that pull toward the final page of the story. The manuscript—the one that had drawn him in, that had consumed him from the moment he laid eyes on it—was not just a book. It was a contract. A binding contract between him and the story. And as the words on the page had begun to shift, to twist, to turn, he had become a part of it. The lines between fiction and reality had blurred, and now there was no escaping.

Evan's mind raced. How could he finish it? What would happen if he did?

"I can't," he whispered, more to himself than the figure. "I can't finish it. If I do, it's over. I'll never get out."

The figure's smile widened, its eyes burning with an intensity that sent a sharp jolt of fear through Evan. "You've always been so afraid of the end," it said softly, almost tenderly. "But the end is inevitable. It's always been inevitable. The story will end, Evan. One way or another."

Evan's stomach twisted. He couldn't breathe. The walls seemed to close in on him as the shadows crept closer, suffocating him, and the manuscript in his hands began to hum with an unnatural energy, as though it were alive, feeding off his fear.

The figure moved closer, its voice now a cold, whispered command. "You will write the ending, Evan. Or the story will write you."

A sudden, violent shiver coursed through Evan's body. He tried to tear his eyes away from the figure, but he couldn't. He couldn't look away. The pull of the manuscript, of the words, was too strong. Every word, every sentence was a thread that tied him to the world he had found himself trapped in. His thoughts were consumed by the desire to finish it. To see the end.

"You are the writer, Evan," the figure repeated, its voice now a low growl. "You are the creator. And this—this is your dilemma.

The story is alive. It's feeding on you. And it will never stop. Unless you finish it."

Evan's mind raced, and for a moment, the weight of the words seemed to crush him. The ending. The ending of the story. If he didn't write it, if he didn't complete it, would he be consumed by it? Would he become part of the pages, trapped forever in this nightmarish world?

The air around him grew thick, oppressive, and Evan could hear the faint whispers again, a constant hum of voices, each one pulling him toward the inevitable. Each one urging him to write, to finish.

He raised the manuscript before him, trembling, his fingers brushing over the words, feeling them shift beneath his touch. And for the first time, he realized something that chilled him to the bone. The manuscript wasn't just a record of the story— it was the story. Every word was alive. Every sentence was a living, breathing entity. And as he read, the words morphed into something else, something darker, something that he couldn't control.

He could hear the figure's voice, cold and merciless in his mind. "You've already started, Evan. You can't stop now."

With a shaking hand, Evan opened the manuscript to the last page. The words on the page were clearer now than they had ever been, their meaning as sharp and cold as a knife's edge.

And then, as his eyes scanned the final sentence, the truth hit him with the force of a freight train:

The writer was never meant to escape. The writer was meant to write.

He had been the one creating this nightmare all along. The words, the pages, the very world around him—he had created it. And now, there was only one thing left to do.

He had to finish the story.

12

The Pen is Mightier

The manuscript burned in Evan's hands, its weight pressing down on him, as though the pages themselves were pulling him deeper into their web. His heart thundered in his chest, each beat a drumbeat of impending doom. The words on the pages, once cryptic, had become clearer, more insistent, more demanding. It was as though the story had developed a mind of its own, and he was no longer just a part of it—he was the center of it.

As his fingers traced the final words of the manuscript, a sharp, cold wind howled through the library, the shelves groaning under the pressure. The smell of old ink and parchment grew stronger, the scent so thick it felt like it was seeping into his very skin. The air itself seemed to vibrate with an unseen energy, a force that tugged at the edges of his consciousness.

"Finish it," the figure whispered, its voice now echoing from every shadow in the room. "You know you must."

Evan's stomach churned, his mind a whirlwind of conflicting thoughts. He could feel the pull, the undeniable desire to complete the story, to bring everything to a close. The final chapter—the end. But with that end came something darker, something far more dangerous than he had ever imagined.

The figure stepped closer, its long, spindly fingers reaching out, its face twisting into something almost familiar, yet foreign. "You don't understand, do you, Evan? You've been writing your own story this whole time. Every word, every sentence. And now... now you must write the final one."

His breath caught in his throat. The weight of the truth pressed down on him like an invisible force. The realization struck him like a lightning bolt—he wasn't just writing the story. He was the story. Every twist, every turn, every character had been created by his own hand, his own thoughts. Even the figure standing before him, the twisted reflection of himself, was his creation. His mind had birthed it all, and now, he had to face the consequences of that creation.

"I can't do it," Evan whispered, his voice raw. "I can't finish it."

The figure chuckled, a sound that made the hairs on the back of Evan's neck stand on end. "You don't have a choice. The story isn't just a story anymore, Evan. It's real. And it's hungry."

The words cut through him like a blade. The story was alive. It had become more than just ink on paper; it had become a force of its own. A force that could no longer be controlled.

Evan's grip tightened on the manuscript, and he could feel it pulse with an energy that was no longer just the words—it was the story itself, alive and waiting for him to give it life. To give it its ending.

The shadows in the room seemed to grow thicker, the edges of the shelves blurring as they stretched toward him, as though the very walls were closing in. The figure's eyes glinted with an eerie satisfaction, as though it had been waiting for this moment. Waiting for Evan to realize the truth.

"You can't escape it, Evan," the figure hissed, stepping forward, its form shifting like smoke. "The pen is mightier than you think. And now, it controls you."

Evan stumbled back, his chest tight, his breath coming in short gasps. He could feel the weight of the manuscript pulling him toward the table, the ink on the pages seeming to glow in the dim light. The words beckoned to him, an irresistible pull, urging him to finish the story.

His hands were shaking, sweat beading on his forehead as his fingers hovered above the last, unfinished sentence. He had no choice. He had to write. He had to finish it.

But what would happen once the story was over? What would become of him?

As though the manuscript could hear his thoughts, the words shifted, twisting before his eyes. They were no longer just written in ink—they were etched into the very air around him, as though they were part of the world itself. Every letter, every line became alive, swirling around him, filling his vision until there was nothing but the words.

His mind was spinning, overwhelmed by the sheer force of the story's power. He could feel the energy of it, the life of it, wrapping around him like a shroud. It wanted to be finished. It wanted to be free.

Evan could hear the figure's voice, now echoing in his mind, urging him to take the final step. "You've written yourself into a corner, Evan. There's no way out. Not for you. Not for anyone."

The air around him grew heavier, and his chest tightened as the words swirled faster, the weight of them pressing down on him, suffocating him. He could no longer think. The manuscript had become an extension of him, the ink on the pages becoming part of his own blood, his own soul. The pull was undeniable.

He opened the book to the last page, his heart hammering in his chest. The figure's voice faded, replaced by the words on the page, which now seemed to writhe with life. He didn't know if it was his own mind, or if the story itself was speaking to him.

The writer who dares to finish the story must be prepared for the consequences.

The final sentence lingered in his mind, its weight almost too much to bear. Evan's hand hovered above the page, his fingers trembling as the manuscript hummed with a quiet, almost malicious energy.

What if finishing it meant he would disappear? What if finishing it meant that the story would consume him whole, leaving nothing behind?

The shadows in the room seemed to whisper, as though they, too, were waiting. Watching. Evan closed his eyes for a moment, his fingers poised above the page. The story was waiting for him to make a choice. His choice.

The weight of his own fear pressed in on him, but the urge to finish—to end it—was overwhelming.

With a sharp inhale, he pressed the pen to the page.

And the world shifted.

In that moment, everything stopped. The air held its breath. The shadows fell silent. The words on the page blurred, then sharpened, then twisted, the ink moving like liquid, swirling on its own, flowing in time with Evan's pulse.

The room seemed to melt away, the shelves disappearing, the walls crumbling into dust. The only thing left was the manuscript—and him.

The figure was gone.

There was only one thing left to do. He wrote. He finished it. The ink bled into the final sentence.

And the story ended.

But Evan wasn't sure if he had written the end—or if the end had written him.

13

The Aftermath

Evan's eyes shot open, his breath coming in ragged gasps. The room was silent. Too silent. He was no longer standing in the grand library, surrounded by endless shelves of ancient, decaying books. There were no shadows creeping toward him. No whispering figure. No eerie hum of energy filling the air.

It was... still.

The manuscript lay in front of him on the cold, wooden table. He reached out slowly, his hand trembling as it hovered above the pages, afraid to touch it, afraid to acknowledge the weight of what he had just done. The pen, which had felt so heavy in his hand only moments ago, now lay abandoned beside it, as if it had been forgotten, discarded.

For a long moment, Evan couldn't move. He just sat there, frozen, staring at the manuscript. His mind was a blank canvas, painted over with the sheer force of the story's finality.

Had he really finished it? Had he truly ended the nightmare?

Tentatively, he lifted the book, his fingers brushing against the cover. The texture was still cold to the touch, but there was something different about it now. Something that made his skin crawl. The air around him felt thicker, more oppressive, as if it were clinging to him, waiting for him to understand something. Waiting for him to realize that the story wasn't truly over.

His heart raced as he opened the pages. The words were the same, the sentences clear and coherent, just as they had been when he first set his hands on them. There was no sign of any distortion. No lingering madness, no sense of something unfinished. It looked... normal. Too normal. But as his eyes scanned the lines, a strange sense of dread crept over him.

He should have felt relief. He should have felt liberated. He had escaped the torment of the story, the suffocating pressure that had driven him into madness. But all he felt now was a growing sense of unease.

The shadows in the room, which had seemed to vanish when he completed the manuscript, began to reappear. Not as dark, writhing shapes, but as subtle distortions in the space around him. He could see them creeping at the edges of his vision, gathering in the corners of the room, like something waiting just outside of his awareness.

Evan closed the book with a snap, his mind screaming at him to look away, to ignore the strange sensation that was gnawing at the edges of his perception. But he couldn't. His eyes were drawn to the last page. The last sentence. He had written it, hadn't he? He had finished the story. But the words were now calling to him.

He opened the book again. The page… the final page… was no longer empty.

The words that had been there, the ones that had marked the end of the story, were gone.

No, not gone, he realized, his breath catching in his throat. They were shifting. They were changing. The letters twisted and morphed, rearranging themselves like a living thing. It was as though the story was rewriting itself, like a twisted reflection in a broken mirror.

The final sentence, the one that should have ended everything, was now a new sentence. A new sentence that Evan couldn't quite read. His eyes strained, but the words blurred, spinning on the page as if they were mocking him. His head swam, and for a fleeting moment, the room seemed to spin with the force of it.

And then, from the corners of the room, the whispering started again.

At first, it was faint. A soft hiss in the distance, like wind moving through cracks in the walls. But then it grew louder. Closer. The voices were coming from every direction, filling his ears, filling his head, until he could no longer tell if the sound was real or if it was inside his mind.

"You cannot escape," they whispered in unison. "You cannot escape the story."

Evan's eyes widened. The figure—the one that had haunted him, the one that had urged him to finish the manuscript—was no longer just a memory. It was real. It was here.

The shadows shifted in front of him, pooling around the edges of the room, taking shape, coalescing into a form that was too familiar, too terrifying. The figure stepped out from the darkness, its twisted smile wide and unrelenting.

"You thought you could escape," it said, its voice dripping with mockery, "but there is no escape from the story, Evan. You are the story. You are the creator, the writer, the architect. And now..." it paused, a grin spreading across its face, "now you will be the subject."

Evan's breath caught in his throat. He knew. He understood now. The story had never been finished. It had only begun. He had been the one to write it, but it was writing him. The figure had known all along, had led him down this path, knowing that the end was never truly the end.

"You are trapped in the very words you've written," the figure continued, its form shifting like smoke. "Every character you've created, every plot you've crafted—they are not separate from you. They are you. They are part of you. And now, you must live with them. Forever."

Evan's pulse quickened. His mind raced, but no answers came.

The room closed in around him, the shadows pressing forward like dark hands reaching for him. He could feel them tugging at his soul, pulling him deeper into the story, into the web that he had woven. The manuscript, the book in his hands, was no longer just a collection of words. It was alive. It was a force, a being that was feeding on him, on his fear, on his doubt.

His fingers clenched around the pages, the weight of it like an anchor pulling him into a sea of darkness. His mind screamed for him to stop, to rip the book apart, to run. But there was nowhere to run. No escape.

The figure's grin widened, its eyes glowing with a malevolent light. "You think you are the writer, but you are only a character. You are bound by the words you've written. You are a prisoner of your own making."

The shadows closed in, tightening around him, and for the first time, Evan realized the full horror of what he had done. The story wasn't something he could control. It was him. It was everything he was, everything he had become. And now, there was no escaping it.

The whispers grew louder, the air growing colder as the figure stepped closer, its form blurring into darkness.

Evan could feel it now, the suffocating weight of the manuscript pressing against him, pushing him deeper into the story. He wasn't just in it anymore—he was it. And the story would never let him go.

14

The Writer's Curse

The darkness pressed in around Evan, thick and suffocating. The figure stood before him, a grotesque reflection of his own fears, its twisted form flickering in and out of focus like a broken signal. The shadows beneath it writhed like living things, reaching toward him, pulling at his ankles, trying to drag him into the abyss. He couldn't move. The weight of the manuscript in his hands felt like a deadweight, like it had fused with his skin, an inseparable part of him now.

"Why are you doing this?" Evan's voice cracked as he looked up at the figure. His mind was racing, but there were no words that seemed to make sense. No answers that could explain the nightmare that was unfolding.

The figure smiled, but it wasn't a smile of satisfaction. It was a smile of knowing, of inevitability. It tilted its head slightly, the shadows shifting across its face like a veil.

"You still don't understand, do you, Evan?" The figure's voice echoed, vibrating the walls around him, sending a cold shiver down his spine. "You are the writer, yes. But you are also the written. The story will never let you go. And now..." It stepped closer, its form flickering like a dying flame, "now you are bound to it. Forever."

Evan's chest tightened, his breath coming in shallow gasps. He wanted to scream, to rage, but his body betrayed him. He couldn't move. His arms were locked in place, his hands clutching the manuscript as though it were the only thing keeping him grounded in this terrible reality. But the manuscript was no salvation. It was the source of his torment. The very thing that had ensnared him.

His mind raced back to the moment when he had written the final sentence—the moment when the figure had disappeared, when the room had seemed to collapse in on itself. He had thought he had finished the story. He had thought he had ended it. But in doing so, he had opened a door to something far darker. Something much more insidious than he could have ever imagined.

The figure's voice filled the room again, this time closer, more insistent. "You thought you could write yourself out of this. But you can't, Evan. Every word you've written, every character, every event—it's a trap. You created this world, and now you must live in it."

The walls around him began to tremble, the air growing heavier with every passing second. The shadows coiled around the floor, creeping toward him like serpents, waiting to strike. His heart hammered in his chest, but it was as though time had slowed down. His thoughts moved in slow motion, but his body remained frozen, trapped in this world of his own creation.

"You're trapped," the figure whispered, its voice wrapping around his mind like a vice. "You can't escape. You'll never escape."

Evan's hands clenched around the manuscript, his knuckles turning white. The words on the pages, which had once been his refuge, were now his prison. He could feel the ink seeping into his skin, the lines of the story etching themselves into his very soul. The plot twisted in his mind, repeating over and over again, like an unending loop.

"Please..." he whispered, the word barely escaping his lips. "Please, I didn't mean it. I never meant for this to happen. I just wanted to tell a story."

The figure laughed, a low, mocking sound that seemed to reverberate through the very air. "You don't get to choose, Evan. You never did. You thought you had control over the story, over everything. But in the end, the story controls you."

Evan tried to close the book, to force himself away from it, but his hands were no longer his own. The pages fluttered open on their own accord, the words growing brighter, more vivid. The characters he had written, the ones he had so carefully created, began to take shape in the shadows, emerging from the dark corners of the room.

First came the woman—her long, dark hair flowing like a river of ink, her eyes wide and searching, as though she, too, was lost in this world. Then came the man—the one who had been the antagonist, the one Evan had written into existence to challenge the protagonist. But now, in the dim light, he seemed different. Darker. His eyes glinted with malice, his features twisted in ways Evan hadn't intended.

"Is this what you wanted?" the figure asked, its voice now a low hiss. "To give life to these characters, to trap them in your story? You created them, but they have lives of their own now. They remember. They know what you've done."

Evan's throat went dry, and he looked around the room, his eyes darting from the figures to the manuscript, to the shifting shadows. His mind was a blur, but one thought cut through the chaos: They know.

The woman—the protagonist, the one who had been so inno-cent in the beginning—stepped forward, her eyes locking with Evan's. There was no recognition there. No affection. Only coldness. Only accusation.

"You think you can write your way out of this?" she asked, her voice hollow, empty. "You think you can just erase us? But we're real now. We live, just as you do. And we will not be forgotten."

Evan felt a cold sweat break out across his forehead as the realization hit him like a fist to the gut. He had done this. He had created them. And now, they were alive. Not just on the pages, but in the world. In his world. The world he could no longer escape.

The figure stepped forward, its hand reaching out toward him. "You see now, don't you? You are not just the writer. You are the cursed one. You gave them life, but now you must live with them. You are trapped inside the very story you thought you could control."

Evan's chest tightened as he tried to pull away, but there was nowhere to go. The walls were closing in, the shadows thickening, the figures—his creations—advancing on him, their eyes now glowing with an unnatural light.

"No..." he whispered, the words thick with fear. "No, this can't be happening. I can't be trapped here. I can't..."

"You already are," the figure replied, its voice full of dark satisfaction. "You will never leave. The story lives, and so do you. Bound together. Forever."

Evan tried to scream, but no sound came out. The shadows closed in around him, and the world he had created became the world he could never escape. The story had claimed him, and now he was nothing more than a character, doomed to live out his own creation for all eternity.

And as the darkness consumed him, he realized the cruelest truth of all.

He had never been the writer.

He had always been the written.

15

The Unwritten

The darkness pressed against Evan's chest, suffocating him, drowning him in its cold, relentless grip. The manuscript was still in his hands, though it now felt like it was more a part of him than an object he could control. His fingers trembled as they clutched it, but every attempt to release it was met with an overwhelming force that kept them bound to its weight. The words had long since ceased to be mere ink on paper. They had become something living. Something sentient.

The figures stood before him, their faces blank slates, eyes glowing with a cruel understanding of their creator's fate. They moved around him like specters, ever-shifting, but always within his reach. The woman, the antagonist, and all those in between, their forms weaving in and out of the shadows, like characters who had escaped their roles—no longer confined to the pages, but free to walk in this twisted, half-real world.

Evan tried to speak, tried to shout at them to stop—to end this madness—but no words escaped him. He was trapped, unable to break free from the suffocating grasp of the story. His heart thudded in his chest, and each beat seemed to echo louder in the hollow, oppressive silence of the room.

But then, from the silence, there came a sound—a whisper, faint at first, but growing louder. A voice, unfamiliar, yet strangely comforting in the sea of dread. It was calling his name.

"Evan... Evan..."

The sound of his name in the empty space felt like a lifeline, like a spark in the darkness. He didn't know where it was coming from, but it was there, and it was the first thing to pierce the terror that gripped him. His head snapped toward the source, and for a brief moment, he thought he saw a figure standing just beyond the shadows—a silhouette, barely visible, yet impossibly familiar.

The whisper continued, "Evan, listen to me. You have to find the unwritten."

The words cut through him like a blade. Unwritten? What did that mean? There was no more story left to write. He had finished it. He had written the ending. Hadn't he?

"Find the unwritten," the voice repeated, more urgent now. "Before it's too late."

Evan's pulse quickened. He looked around, trying to locate the source of the voice, but the room around him was distorted—pulsing, breathing, shifting in a way that defied reality. The characters that surrounded him were no longer just figures from his story; they were alive, their eyes now filled with an unsettling hunger. The woman, the antagonist, and even the minor characters—they were all moving toward him, their expressions twisted into grim mockeries of what they once had been.

They knew. They knew he was trying to break free. And they were coming for him.

Evan's body was frozen, unable to react, but his mind was racing. The voice. It had to be the key. But how? How could he escape when every moment of his existence was written in the pages of the manuscript? Was there something he had missed? Some part of the story that had been left out, something he hadn't considered?

The shadows closed in around him, thickening, pressing against him, and Evan could feel the weight of their malice. It was like being suffocated by his own creations.

"Find the unwritten, Evan."

The voice was louder now, and this time, it felt like it was coming from within him. He closed his eyes, trying to concentrate on the words. Find the unwritten. What did it mean? How could he find something that wasn't there?

And then, as if in response to his question, something inside him stirred. A memory, buried deep beneath the weight of his fear, rose to the surface. The first time he had picked up the pen, before the manuscript had taken on a life of its own. Before the story had consumed him. There had been an idea, a fleeting thought, something that hadn't made it into the narrative. A thread left hanging, a possibility that had never been explored.

The unwritten.

His eyes snapped open, and for the first time in what felt like forever, he felt a flicker of clarity. The voice wasn't just telling him to find something physical. It was telling him to look inside, to find the part of himself that had been erased by the story. The part of him that still had control.

The figures around him advanced, their movements deliberate, closing in like predators on their prey. The woman—the protagonist—smiled cruelly as she approached, her eyes glinting with malice. "You think you can escape us, Evan?" she taunted. "You created us. You are nothing without us."

Evan's breath hitched, but something within him shifted. He felt it—a small, quiet rebellion against the words, against the plot that had bound him. The story had taken everything from him. His identity. His freedom. But it hadn't taken everything. It hadn't taken this.

The manuscript. The words. They were his to command. He had created them, yes. But they had also been shaped by him. They were not gods. They were not all-powerful. They were mere reflections of his thoughts. His will. And now, for the first time, he realized that he didn't have to follow the script. He could change it.

The shadows that had once consumed him recoiled as he focused on the idea. The unwritten. The space between the lines. The breath before the next word. It was there—waiting for him to reach it.

The air around him began to hum, vibrating with a strange energy as the manuscript trembled in his hands. He felt the words, the very pages themselves, pushing against him. It was as if they were alive, resisting him, trying to drag him back into the confines of the story. But Evan pushed harder, focusing on that space—the unwritten.

With a surge of determination, he spoke, his voice shaking but clear. "I will write you."

The figures froze, their expressions faltering, their movements stilled as if they were waiting for something. A breath. A shift. The world seemed to pause for an instant.

Evan took a step back, then another, and the room began to shift with him, the walls warping, the air bending, as though his very will was rewriting the space around him. The shadows twisted, recoiling from him, unable to hold him anymore. The manuscript began to glow faintly, the words on the pages shifting, rearranging, as though something—someone—was rewriting them from the inside out.

The woman—the protagonist—reached out for him, but her fingers turned to dust before they could touch him. The antagonist snarled, his form flickering in and out of existence, but even he began to fade, his power weakening, undone by

Evan's refusal to stay confined within the story.

Evan's heart pounded as he felt himself slip between worlds, between the written and the unwritten. The darkness that had once threatened to consume him began to retreat, unraveling in the face of his will.

But it wasn't over. Not yet.

The manuscript still pulsed in his hands, its weight shifting between freedom and imprisonment. And the voice—the unwritten voice—continued to whisper, urging him on.

You've started something, Evan. But the story is never truly finished. It will follow you. It will always find you.

Evan's grip tightened on the pages, his mind now clear. He had broken free. But only just.

And in that fleeting moment of victory, he knew one thing for certain:

There was no such thing as an unwritten world.

Not for him. Not anymore.

16

The Echo of Fate

The cold air was thick with the scent of ink. Evan felt it fill his lungs, but it wasn't just a smell. It was a sensation, a memory locked deep within his chest. The pages of the manuscript had stopped glowing, but they still pulsed with a quiet, eerie energy, as if the words were alive, waiting. He could feel them pressing against his palms, twisting, changing, bending in ways that shouldn't be possible.

He couldn't breathe.

The world around him shimmered, the edges of reality blurring and warping, but it wasn't the chaos of the shadows from before. It was something else. Something more familiar. A feeling that made the hairs on the back of his neck rise in warning.

The figures, the characters—his creations—were gone. The room was empty, save for him and the manuscript. But the silence was deafening.

Suddenly, a low hum filled the air, like the distant sound of something far too large to be ignored. Evan looked around, but the sound didn't seem to come from any direction. It came from inside him, a vibration that resonated deep within his chest.

The manuscript... it was vibrating, pulsing more intensely now, as though it had a heartbeat of its own. A strange heat radiated from the pages, and despite every instinct telling him to drop it, to run, Evan felt an undeniable pull to the book. He couldn't explain it. He didn't understand it. But he had to know what would happen next. He had to understand why he couldn't escape.

As his fingers brushed the pages, a single word stood out, its ink shifting with a life of its own, flickering before his eyes. It was the word he hadn't seen before. The word that hadn't been there when he wrote the story, the word that had appeared after the shadows receded.

"Fate."

The word rippled across the pages, and then the sound—louder now—crashed into him. A sound like thunder, yet softer, like a distant scream, reverberating in his skull. His head throbbed, his vision blurring, and he staggered backward, the manuscript slipping from his fingers. But it wasn't gone. It was still there, on the floor, but it was no longer just a book. The pages were stretching, folding outward, expanding as if the book itself were growing, consuming the space around it.

And then, in the center of it, something began to form.

A figure.

At first, it was nothing more than a blur—just a shadow in the center of the pages—but it quickly solidified, rising from the manuscript as if it had been trapped within the ink all along. Evan's heart slammed in his chest. It was the figure—the one he hadn't written. The one that had always been missing, the one that had whispered to him in the darkness. The embodiment of fate.

It was an image he knew all too well, though he had never consciously created it. It was the reflection of his own self—his own face—but there was something darker, something wrong in its eyes. Its presence felt like a weight on his soul, like a crushing inevitability that could not be undone. It wore his face, but it wasn't him. It was the version of himself that would never be free, the one chained to the words on the page, bound by destiny.

It smiled.

And Evan could feel his mind unraveling at the edges. A wave of terror swept over him, drowning out every thought, every instinct to fight. It was fate—manifested in a form he could no longer escape. His creation, his reflection, had come to life.

"You think you can outrun me?" the figure spoke, its voice low, twisted, as if it echoed from every corner of the universe, bouncing off the walls of his mind. "I am the thread you cannot sever, the ending you cannot rewrite. You cannot escape me. You will never escape me."

Evan's legs buckled beneath him, and he collapsed to the floor, his head spinning. The figure took a slow, deliberate step forward, its feet barely touching the ground, as though it were walking on air. Its eyes—those dark, empty eyes—burned into Evan's soul, piercing through the remnants of his will.

"You believed you could control this," it continued, its voice dripping with cruel amusement. "You believed that you could rewrite your fate, but I am the one who controls the ink. The words you write are nothing but echoes of my design."

Evan wanted to scream, to run, to do anything, but he couldn't move. He was paralyzed, locked in place by the overwhelming presence of the figure. His body betrayed him, the fear too thick to push through. The figure stepped closer, its shadow stretching over him, its smile growing wider, more sinister.

"Every character, every plot twist, every turn you thought was your decision—was mine," it said, crouching down until its face was level with his. "You cannot change what has already been written. You cannot fight what is already fated. I am the ink that bleeds through the pages, the fate that haunts your every thought. And you, Evan, are nothing more than a pawn in my story."

Evan gasped for air, his chest constricting with every word. He could feel the weight of the manuscript pressing on him, the ink seeping into his skin, and he realized—too late—that the story had never been his to control. The manuscript wasn't just a book. It was a prison. A prison that held him captive, one word at a time. Each sentence, each page, each chapter had only drawn him deeper into its clutches.

The figure reached out, its fingers cold as they brushed against his forehead, and Evan felt his thoughts blur, his memories twisting like fragile threads in a storm. The story had always been set. There was no escape.

"Your fate was written the moment you picked up the pen," the figure whispered, its breath cold against Evan's ear. "And you will live it. Over and over again. Until the ink runs dry."

The words echoed in his mind, reverberating through every cell in his body. And as they did, he felt something shift— a hollowing sensation, as though his very essence was being drawn out of him, fed to the pages of the manuscript. His body was no longer his own. It was a part of the story, just as much as the characters, just as much as the plot. He had become the ink. He had become the echo.

And when he looked up, the figure was gone.

But it wasn't over.

The manuscript remained, the words waiting for him. And in that silence, Evan understood. The echo of fate would never let him go. It would follow him through every chapter, through every word, until the story was finished. Until he was finished.

There was no end. Not for him. Not for anyone trapped within the ink.

There was only the echo.

17

The Price of Rebellion

Evan's mind swirled with chaos, each thought unraveling faster than he could hold onto them. The figure—his reflection, his fate—had vanished as quickly as it had appeared, but its words remained. They echoed in the hollow space of his thoughts, reverberating, suffocating. There was no escape. There was only the manuscript. Only the story. And he was its captive.

His hands, still trembling, reached for the manuscript again. But as his fingers brushed the pages, a violent jolt shot through him, a searing pain that burned through his veins. The book was no longer just a book. It had become a tether—a cord that connected him to something far darker than he had ever imagined.

The words on the pages began to blur and shift again, but this time, there was no question. They were not his words anymore. They had been stolen. Torn from him. Rewritten.

His chest tightened, and his breath caught in his throat. He was too late. The rebellion—the brief moment when he had taken control—had been nothing more than a fleeting illusion. A momentary crack in the fabric of the story, easily erased by the very thing he had created.

The manuscript began to hum again, but this time it wasn't a soft vibration. It was a pulse, a heartbeat, thundering in time with his own. And through the sound, a voice whispered—a voice that was not his own, yet it felt as though it had always been there, lurking beneath the surface.

"You thought you could change fate," it taunted, its tone dark and knowing. "You thought you could rewrite the story. But there is a price for rebellion."

Evan gasped, recoiling as the words formed in the air around him, their ink dripping like liquid poison. The room around him began to shift, warping as though the very walls were bending to the will of the manuscript. He could feel the presence of the story, thick and suffocating, closing in on him, suffocating him from all sides.

"The price of rebellion," the voice continued, this time filling the space with its presence, making the air feel dense and heavy. "You will never be free, Evan. You will always be bound to me. To the story. To the ink that runs through your veins."

He stumbled backward, but the walls—once mere shadows— now seemed to pulse with life. The floor beneath him cracked and groaned, splitting apart as if something deep below was awakening. And as the cracks spread, the ground seemed to shift—miles of labyrinthine tunnels stretching beneath him, rising to meet him with the undeniable pull of something ancient.

The manuscript in his hands burned with unbearable heat. His skin seared where the pages touched him, and he dropped it to the floor, stepping away as if the book itself was trying to pull him back into its grip.

But as he looked down, he saw something he hadn't noticed before.

A figure, barely visible at first, stood within the darkened corners of the room. It was tall, its limbs long and skeletal, its silhouette distorted by the shadows. The air around it seemed to warp, as if it were an extension of the darkness itself. Evan's heart slammed in his chest as he realized what it was.

It was another character. One he hadn't written.

And yet, it felt like he had.

The figure stepped forward, its eyes glowing faintly in the dim light. It was a reflection of something far more sinister than anything he could have ever imagined. Its movements were jerky, unnatural, as if it had not yet found its form.

"You will never escape me, Evan," it rasped, its voice a hollow whisper. "I am the price of your rebellion."

Evan's mind screamed. He knew this—knew it. He had felt it

before, deep within the manuscript. The other side of the story. The part that no one was meant to see. The price of altering fate, of changing the words that were never meant to be touched.

The figure's limbs contorted in impossible angles, twisting unnaturally as it drew closer. "You thought you could rewrite your ending, but you can't change what's already been etched. Every word, every plot, is mine. And now, you will pay for thinking otherwise."

The air around Evan grew heavier, and the edges of the room seemed to blur again. The figure moved like a storm, faster now, more determined. It was not a creature born from the pages. It was a creation born from the consequence of rebellion. A punishment for those who dared to alter the course of the story. A manifestation of the story's will.

The walls began to close in, and the floor cracked open beneath his feet. Evan stumbled backward, his breath coming in short gasps. There was nowhere to go. Nowhere to hide. The manuscript still lay on the ground, its pages turning on their own, feeding the chaos around him.

"You are mine now," the figure said, its voice louder, more insistent, as it drew closer. Its shape was becoming clearer, more distinct, but that only made it more terrifying. Its features were twisted, not quite human, but familiar in a way that made Evan's stomach churn. "You thought you could escape me by changing the story. But the story does not bend. It does not break. And now, you will be its prisoner forever."

Evan's mind reeled. He had seen this before. He had felt it when he picked up the pen. The characters. The plot. The words. All of it had been set. He had known, deep down, that there would be a cost for trying to rewrite fate. But he hadn't believed it.

Now, there was no escape. He was caught in the story's web, trapped between the ink and the consequences of his own actions. The figure—his own creation—moved toward him, its shadow swallowing the room, its presence overpowering every instinct within him.

"No," Evan whispered, more to himself than to the figure. "I won't be a part of this."

The figure's smile grew wider, colder, as it reached out for him. Its fingers elongated, the nails sharp and glinting like knives. "You have no choice. You never did."

Evan took a step back, his pulse pounding in his ears. His chest was tight, his vision swimming, but he knew he couldn't give in. Not yet.

There had to be a way. There had to be a way to fight back, to escape the price he had paid for rebellion. He had written the story. He had created this nightmare, but that also meant he could destroy it. He could burn it all down.

His fingers grazed the edges of the manuscript, and he felt the words crawling up his skin, like a fire racing beneath his flesh. The price of rebellion was not just his life—it was his very soul.

But as the figure reached for him, its long fingers curling into the air, Evan knew one thing for certain:

The story could not end until he chose.

And the choice, the price, was his to make.

18

The Pen's Shadow

Evan's heart thundered in his chest, his every breath shallow as the figure loomed before him. The weight of its presence pressed down on him, suffocating him, as if the very air around him was being stolen. The room had collapsed into an abyss, the walls now stretching and twisting like the folds of an ancient, haunted manuscript, bending reality itself.

He could still feel the manuscript beneath his fingers, but it no longer felt like a lifeline. It was a trap. The words pulsed with a malicious energy, pulling him deeper into their dark embrace. With every passing moment, the pages of the manuscript turned on their own, each page a reminder of the fate he had unwittingly sealed when he first dared to pick up the pen.

The figure—the creature born of his rebellion—hovered in the space before him, its limbs distorting, its body twisting unnaturally as it reached out. Its eyes, dark voids that seemed to consume the very light in the room, locked onto Evan with a relentless, piercing stare. There was no escape, no way out of the nightmare he had unleashed.

"You cannot change the course of fate," the figure intoned, its voice a chilling whisper that scraped against his mind, like nails on a chalkboard. "The story has already been written. And now you will be the ink that seals it."

Evan staggered backward, his legs unsteady beneath him. His mind screamed at him to move, to run, but his body betrayed him. Every instinct, every warning from deep within, told him that the creature in front of him was the embodiment of the very thing he had tried to defy—the inexorable march of destiny, the unyielding power of the written word.

He could feel it, the story, binding him. The manuscript's ink had seeped under his skin, into his veins, and now, he was a part of it. He was no longer just its creator. He was its prisoner.

A cold, bitter laugh echoed in the air, sending a shiver down his spine. The figure moved closer, its face shifting, its features warping in a grotesque dance of shadows and light. It was mocking him, enjoying the terror that twisted his insides.

"You thought the pen was your tool," it hissed. "But it was never yours to control. You were always its servant. And now, it's time to pay the price."

The figure raised its hand, and the air around Evan seemed to distort as though the space itself was bending in response to its power. A wave of nausea crashed over him, and his vision blurred. He could feel the manuscript's presence tightening around him, suffocating him, until it was the only thing he could see, the only thing he could feel.

His fingers, trembling with desperation, grasped at the book, pulling it close to his chest as if trying to shield himself from the storm of darkness that was closing in. But the manuscript pulsed with a strange, insistent rhythm. Its words were no longer just ink on paper—they were alive, crawling, shifting. They had become a part of him.

And then, the room went still.

The figure stopped moving, its form frozen in place as if waiting. As if watching.

Evan's heart skipped a beat. A single word rang through his mind, louder than any other thought, more powerful than any voice that had spoken to him before:

Rewrite.

The word was a command. A whisper in the depths of his mind, a single thread that had somehow broken through the overwhelming power of the manuscript. It was the key, the flickering possibility of a choice. A choice that he hadn't known existed until now.

His eyes darted around the room, looking for something—anything—that could help him. The walls were closing in again, the shadows wrapping around him like a vice, but in the corner of his vision, a faint glimmer caught his attention. A sliver of light, breaking through the darkness. A pen.

The pen, the one he had used to write the story, lay discarded on the ground, its silver surface catching what little light there was. It was just a pen—nothing special, nothing more than an instrument of his own creation.

But now, it felt like something more. Something important.

With a surge of desperation, Evan reached for it. The moment his fingers wrapped around its cool, smooth surface, the world seemed to pause. For an instant, everything was still. The air itself held its breath, as if waiting for his next move.

The figure, still motionless, seemed to watch him, its cold eyes never leaving his face.

Evan's pulse raced, his mind spinning with the weight of the decision. He knew what this meant. If he picked up the pen again, if he wrote...

It would all change.

But what would he write? What could he possibly write that would give him the power to escape the nightmare he had created? The manuscript was no longer just his story—it was a living thing. It had its own will, its own desire to consume everything he loved, everything he was.

He could feel the weight of the manuscript in his hands, pulling him toward it. The pen was an extension of his mind, but now it was more—much more. It was the only weapon he had left.

A choice.

With a tremor in his hand, Evan lifted the pen. He held it above the manuscript, the ink swirling on the pages as if it, too, knew what was coming.

"You cannot escape," the figure said again, its voice a low growl. "The ink will never let you go."

The words burned in his mind, but Evan gritted his teeth. He had no choice. If he didn't take control now, if he didn't rewrite the story, there would be no escaping the fate that awaited him. No escaping the creature that stood before him.

He closed his eyes, took a deep breath, and began to write.

The pen moved with fluidity, the words flowing from his mind as if they were meant to be there. Each stroke felt like a battle, a fight against the dark force that had taken root in his soul. The manuscript trembled in his hands as the ink spilled across the pages.

And then—

A jolt.

A pulse of pure, unrelenting power surged through his body, and the world shattered.

The room collapsed into darkness, and Evan was no longer in control.

The pen had written something new. Something that neither he nor the figure could have ever anticipated.

A price had been paid. A new story was beginning.

19

The Ink's Rebellion

Evan's eyes snapped open, but the world before him was no longer the one he had known. The room was gone. The manuscript was gone. Everything had dissolved into a vast, unending darkness that stretched endlessly in every direction. He felt weightless, suspended in the middle of nowhere, as if the very concept of space had ceased to exist. He could hear nothing but the frantic beat of his own heart in his chest, pounding relentlessly, as though it, too, had become part of the void.

But something was there. Something more.

It was a presence. A familiar one. Cold, suffocating, watching. And it wasn't alone.

The figure. The creature that had once loomed in the room with him, its distorted, skeletal form lingering in the shadows, now stood at the edges of the void, its eyes glowing brighter than before, more intense, more powerful.

It was different.

The figure moved toward him, its limbs elongating with each step, stretching and bending at unnatural angles as if the fabric of reality itself couldn't contain it. It was no longer a shadow or a manifestation. It was real. It was alive, and it was furious.

"You should have known," the figure rasped, its voice a horrible, distorted version of its own. The sound rattled Evan's bones, vibrating through him, making every part of him ache. "You thought you could rewrite me. Rewrite us. But the ink... the ink never forgets. And neither do I."

Evan tried to move, but his body wouldn't respond. The weight of the darkness pressed down on him, holding him in place, locking him in this eternal space. His hands twitched, but they could barely form a fist, let alone grab the pen he had once held so tightly. His vision flickered, and the pen—his only hope, his last weapon—vanished from his mind, as though the darkness itself had erased it.

"There was a price," the figure continued, its smile stretching wider, its teeth sharp and jagged. "And now it's time for you to pay."

The ground beneath him rippled, like liquid, and before he could react, the air was torn open. Words. Uncontrollable, frantic words swarmed the darkness, spilling from every corner, every crack in the void. They weren't just words—no, they were the story, taking form, twisting, reshaping, pulling Evan into their grasp.

He felt it before he saw it. The words had become tangible. They were alive, reaching for him with gnashing teeth made of ink, claws of paper, chains of sentences that wrapped around his limbs, his throat, his heart. The very essence of the manuscript had turned against him, its words now seeking retribution for his rebellion.

"No!" Evan gasped, his chest tightening as the words continued to writhe, crawl, and coil around him. "This wasn't supposed to happen. I changed it. I changed it! I re-wrote it!"

The figure's laugh echoed through the void, and Evan could feel his mind unraveling. "Fool," it spat, its voice dripping with venom. "You can't rewrite fate. Not now. Not ever. I am the story. I am the ink, the page, the ending. And I will never let you go."

The words, once fragments of ideas and fragments of Evan's own creation, now surged with an unearthly power. They were no longer just letters and symbols—they were forces, living, breathing entities that had a will of their own.

Evan was trapped.

But then—something shifted. A crack.

A faint sliver of light appeared in the distance, far beyond the dark abyss. It was weak at first, but as Evan focused, it grew brighter, more defined. His heart quickened. Could it be? Was there hope?

The words constricted around him, tightening their grip. The ink burned like fire, scorching his skin, but Evan ignored the pain. He focused on the light, forcing his mind to break through the suffocating grip of the manuscript.

He had rewritten once. He had changed the course of the story. And there was no reason why he couldn't do it again. The ink may have rebelled, but so could he.

The words clawed at his chest, dragging him toward the darkness, but Evan dug deep, reaching into the very core of himself. No. He wouldn't succumb to this. Not again.

With a fierce scream, he pushed against the force of the ink, a surge of willpower flowing through him. His mind, now clearer than ever, focused on the one thing that could shatter the manuscript's hold over him. The story. The words. His words.

He began to write. It wasn't with a pen. It was with his thoughts, his heart, his soul. The ink, the words that had once been a prison, became his weapon.

The sliver of light flared, expanding as his will collided with the dark force. The words writhed and twisted, resisting, but Evan's mind burned brighter, sharper, than ever before. Every stroke he made, every thought he had, pushed against the manuscript's grip.

"No," he whispered, his voice hoarse but determined. "I'm not your prisoner."

The darkness screeched, its voice now a cacophony of thousands of conflicting sounds, all distorted and broken. The figure screamed in fury, but it was powerless against Evan's defiance. The manuscript's grip loosened, the ink no longer a binding chain but a fading memory, its power waning as Evan took control once more.

The light exploded, flooding the void with a blinding radiance. The figure screeched, its form flickering, unraveling, as Evan's mind, now clear and sharp, tore through the darkness. The words that had once bound him to this world, this nightmare, dissolved into dust.

Evan fell to his knees, gasping for air, his hands shaking violently as he realized what had just happened. He had done it. He had rewritten the story again—not just for himself, but for everyone.

The figure was gone. The darkness was fading. And in its place, there was something new. Something he had never expected.

The story was no longer his to control. It was no longer just a creation, a thing to bend and twist at his will. It had taken on a life of its own, one far more powerful than anything he could ever have imagined.

The price of rebellion had been paid, but now, the story would have its own say.

And Evan would have to face the consequences of his own creation.

20

The Echo of Ink

Evan's breath came in ragged gasps as he stared at the blank pages before him. The world had shifted again. He wasn't sure where he was anymore—or even if he was still there—but the air around him hummed with an unnatural energy. The weight of it, thick and suffocating, pressed down on him, as if the very space had grown sentient and was watching, waiting, for something to unfold.

The manuscript lay on the floor before him, its pages fluttering as if caught in an unseen wind. He had thought he'd freed himself. He had thought that by rewriting the story, by breaking the bonds of fate, he could escape the hell that had been created. But the manuscript wasn't gone. It was still here, still waiting for him to return to it.

But this was different.

The ink that had once been a prison, a force that sought to control him, now pulsed with a strange, eerie rhythm. It was as though the manuscript had its own heartbeat, its own life force, and it was alive.

The shadows in the room shifted, twisting like living things, crawling along the walls, stretching toward him as though they, too, were bound by the same dark force that had once held him prisoner. A cold wind swept through the room, though no windows were open. It whispered his name—faintly at first, like a forgotten memory, then louder, insistent, a voice made of a thousand hushed breaths.

"Evan..."

He froze, a chill crawling down his spine. He hadn't heard that voice in what felt like an eternity, but it was unmistakable. He knew it as well as he knew his own. The voice of the manuscript. The voice of the story he had created.

The pages of the manuscript flipped wildly, a frantic, almost desperate sound, as though they were struggling to be freed from their own weight. The words shifted on the page, blurring and re-forming in ways that made no sense. Sentences twisted, paragraphs re-arranged, and then—just as quickly—they disappeared. But the page wasn't empty. There, in the place where the words should have been, there was something more.

A shape.

A figure—more shadow than substance—appeared within the ink, like a reflection in dark water. It was hard to make out, at first, just an outline, but then it took shape: a human form, but distorted, almost grotesque, with eyes too wide and a mouth that stretched too far. It was him—or, at least, it looked like him. But this figure... it wasn't Evan anymore. It was something else.

And then, with an almost imperceptible shift, the figure began to speak.

"Why did you think you could escape me?" the figure asked, its voice a distorted version of his own, layered with whispers that seemed to come from a thousand directions at once. The sound was suffocating, pressing against his ears, filling his head until it felt as though it might explode.

Evan's legs trembled as he tried to take a step back, but he was rooted to the spot. The figure's eyes locked onto his, hollow, endless, voids that seemed to pierce through him. "You thought you could rewrite me. But the story doesn't bend to your will. It never has. It never will."

The figure's mouth stretched into a cruel, knowing smile. It reached out toward the manuscript, and as it did, the pages seemed to fold in on themselves, sucking the figure in, melding with it, until it became part of the ink itself.

Evan's pulse quickened, his hands shaking. "No... this can't be happening..."

He reached down to touch the pages, and as his fingers brushed the ink, he felt it. It was cold. The ink was cold, and it burned.

"Don't touch it," the voice whispered, no longer his own. "It will swallow you whole."

Evan jerked his hand away, but it was too late. The ink had already begun to climb his skin, creeping up his wrist, curling like tendrils of darkness, leaving behind a cold, clammy sensation as it spread. He could feel it, pulsing beneath the surface of his skin, the words written on him now, etched into his very soul.

A laugh echoed around him, hollow and empty. "You wrote the words. You created the world. But now, you are the story. And it will never let you go."

Evan's breath hitched. The room began to close in around him, the walls pressing in, the ceiling lowering with every second. His heart pounded in his chest as the manuscript, the story, consumed everything. It filled the room with its shadow, turning the air thick with its presence. The lines of the words seemed to bleed out from the pages, swirling like ink in water, bending and twisting, merging into one giant pool of darkness.

"Get out," he whispered to himself, panic seizing him. "Get out..."

But the walls—no, the very space—seemed to respond to the story, to the ink, to the words that had been written. They shifted, transformed, and before Evan could react, the room had vanished.

He was falling.

Falling through a void of ink and darkness, his body weightless, the pull of the manuscript dragging him further down. The words flashed by him, swirling, flashing, reshaping into forms he couldn't quite comprehend. It felt like being trapped inside the story, his body and mind disintegrating, becoming part of it.

Suddenly, the fall stopped. He was standing, his feet planted on solid ground, but the world around him was different. The room was gone. He was in a different place now—a place made entirely of ink and shadow. The floor was soft beneath his feet, as if it were made of paper. The air smelled faintly of dust, of old, forgotten things.

The figure—the distorted version of himself—appeared again, standing before him, its face twisted into a grotesque parody of Evan's own. "Do you see now?" it asked, its voice dripping with mockery. "This is what you've done. This is what you've become."

The figure reached out a hand toward him, and with a sickening crack, the ink beneath Evan's feet shifted, and suddenly, he was falling again—this time, not into darkness, but into the very heart of the story itself.

The pages—his story—were waiting.

And there was no way out.

21

The Heart of the Story

Evan awoke with a jolt. The sensation of falling had been replaced by a stifling stillness, an unnatural calm that seemed to press in on him from all sides. His body was sore, aching as if he'd been lying motionless for hours. His limbs felt heavy, like they were trapped in concrete. He blinked rapidly, struggling to clear the fog from his mind, but the world around him refused to focus.

He was no longer in the ink-drenched void he had once known. No, this was different. This was... quieter. The air was thick, heavy, with the scent of something ancient, something forgotten. It smelled like dust, like the pages of an old book left untouched for years. The weight in the air pressed against his chest, suffocating, almost as if the world itself was holding its breath, waiting for something to happen.

Evan tried to move but found his body unresponsive. His hands were glued to the floor—no, not the floor. The floor had vanished, replaced by something that was both familiar and terrifyingly foreign. The ink had seeped into everything, coating the walls, the ground, the ceiling, until it was impossible to tell where one thing ended and another began. The ink had become the world.

As his vision cleared, he saw it: a single, massive book, standing upright in the center of the room. It was enormous, towering over him like a monolith. The cover was plain, black, without any markings to indicate its title. It was the only thing in the room that seemed solid, tangible. Everything else, every inch of the space, was made of swirling ink and darkness, a nightmare of distorted shapes and shifting shadows.

The book beckoned him.

Without thinking, as though his body were moving of its own accord, Evan tried to stand. His legs trembled, and the pain in his joints was unbearable, but he forced himself to his feet, every movement sluggish and laborious. He staggered toward the book, his breath shallow, heart pounding as if it, too, was trying to escape.

The closer he got, the more oppressive the atmosphere became. The shadows seemed to writhe in anticipation, watching him, waiting. Every step felt like a violation, like he was intruding on something ancient, forbidden. But he couldn't stop himself. It was as if the book was pulling him in, urging him to open it.

He reached the massive tome, his fingers brushing the surface of the cover. It was cold. Not just cold like ice, but cold like something that had been buried for centuries, untouched and forgotten. A chill crawled up his spine as his hand hovered over the pages. He wanted to look away, to turn and run, but his fingers moved against his will, pushing open the cover.

The pages inside were blank.

At first, it seemed like a relief. He was used to the twisting, contorting words that had once bound him to this hell. Blankness felt like freedom—like the possibility of an escape. But that relief was short-lived. The longer he stared at the blank pages, the more he felt something shifting, something waiting, hidden beneath the surface. The absence of words was a trap, a silence that rang louder than anything he had ever heard.

Suddenly, the pages began to fill. Slowly at first, then faster, as if they were being written by an invisible hand. Words. Endless, swirling, suffocating words began to bleed onto the paper, appearing in jagged, hurried script. They weren't forming sentences—at least, not sentences that made sense. They were chaotic, fragmented, disjointed, and they filled the pages faster than Evan could comprehend.

But as the ink spread, the words began to shift, to change. They were no longer random. They were becoming familiar. They were becoming his words.

"No," Evan gasped, stepping back from the book, but his feet were stuck. The shadows had risen from the floor, curling around his ankles, holding him in place. His heart hammered in his chest as the ink from the book began to spill out, dripping from the edges of the pages, pooling onto the floor, and slowly climbing toward him. The words that filled the pages were no longer just text—they were alive, moving, twisting, becoming part of him.

Evan's breath quickened as he recognized them. They were sentences from his own story. The ones he had written. The ones he had tried to escape. He had thought he was free, but now, with the words rushing toward him, he realized the truth. There was no escaping the story. It was him. It had always been him.

"You can't escape me," a voice hissed, not from the book, but from within the ink itself. It was a thousand voices, all distorted, all coming from different directions at once. The voice was everywhere, swirling around him, inside him. "You belong to me. You wrote me. And now... I write you."

The words continued to bleed from the book, now creeping up Evan's legs, wrapping around his body like living tendrils of ink. He could feel it, the weight of the words pressing against him, suffocating him, crawling beneath his skin. His chest tightened as the ink spread, covering his arms, his face, his chest. He tried to scream, but the ink flooded into his mouth, silencing him, choking him, filling his lungs.

The last thing he saw was the book—its pages still filling, still consuming, as his vision darkened and his body froze, trapped by the very words he had written.

And then... silence.

Evan awoke again—this time, not in a room of ink and shadows, but in the place between stories. It was a void, a realm that existed between the folds of the manuscript, where time and space didn't quite function the way they should. It was a place he had never seen before, but he knew instinctively that it was where stories went when they died.

It was where he had gone.

The words—the ink—had stopped. But not completely. There was a whisper, a faint echo, that echoed through the empty void. A name. His name.

"Evan..."

He spun around, his pulse quickening. The voice sounded distant, but he could feel it, deep inside, like it was coming from the very core of the story. The story that had him now. The story that had become him.

"You thought you could control it," the voice murmured, and Evan knew then, without a doubt, that the story was no longer his to command. "You were never the author, Evan. You were always just part of the plot."

And as the voice faded into the darkness, Evan realized the truth. The heart of the story wasn't the manuscript. It wasn't the ink or the words.

It was him.

And he would never escape.

22

The Silence That Screams

Evan woke in darkness. He could feel it before his eyes even opened—an oppressive weight pressing in from every direction, like the very air had become thick with dread. His body was stiff, cold, as if he had been lying motionless for years, frozen in time. He couldn't remember how he had gotten here or where here even was, but the emptiness around him was more than just a lack of light. It was a complete absence of everything—a void that seemed to absorb all sound, all movement, all meaning.

He tried to speak, but the words wouldn't come. His mouth was dry, as though it had been sealed shut, his throat tight, constricting with an unspoken pressure. He felt like he was suffocating, but there was no air to struggle for, no breath to be taken.

The darkness pressed in around him, more suffocating than the silence. And yet, in that silence, there was a noise—a faint, subtle sound, so quiet it could almost be ignored, but Evan knew it was there. A whisper. It was as though the darkness itself was speaking to him, calling him, beckoning him closer to something he couldn't see, couldn't understand. He couldn't escape it.

The sound grew louder. The whisper was joined by another, then another, until the air itself was thick with the hum of voices that didn't quite belong to anyone. They whispered his name.

"Evan..."

His name, spoken in a thousand different tones, overlapping one another, each one more insistent than the last. Each one more desperate. He jerked his head from side to side, trying to locate the source of the voices, but there was nothing. Nothing but the silence that screamed in his ears, deafening in its intensity.

His heartbeat quickened as the whispers grew louder, more demanding. He tried to rise, to push himself off the cold ground beneath him, but his limbs felt heavy, unresponsive. He could barely move, like he was trapped in a dream, unable to break free.

"Evan... you can't run from us..."

The words hit him like a punch to the gut. He froze. The voice was different this time, darker, more familiar. It was a voice he had heard before—a voice from the story, a voice that had been chasing him from the very beginning. The voice that had created him, that had trapped him in the web of its words.

"You are mine," the voice continued, low and smooth, like a serpent coiling around his thoughts. "You have always been mine."

Evan's breath caught in his throat. "No... no, I'm not yours. I—"

The voice cut him off. "You don't get to choose, Evan. You never did."

The whispers grew louder, swirling around him, pressing against his skull. It was as though the darkness itself had come alive, had turned into a living, breathing entity that sought to devour him. The shadows were closing in, and Evan could feel them—not just surrounding him, but inside him, moving through his veins, slipping into his mind. He could feel the words of the story crawling through his skin, twisting through his thoughts, wrapping around his consciousness until there was nothing left but the story's will.

He gasped for air, but there was none. The darkness was suffocating him, pushing against his chest, holding him captive. He had to move, had to escape—but where could he go? He had no idea which direction was up or down, left or right. It was all the same here. Everything was the same.

A cold, bitter laugh echoed through the void. "You think you can escape me?" The voice was mocking, cruel. "You can't escape yourself. Not this time. You are the story, Evan. You have always been the story."

Evan's body trembled, his legs buckling beneath him. He dropped to his knees, his hands clutching his head as if he could force the voices out. But it only made them louder.

"You wrote the words," the voice whispered. "And now the words own you."

He wanted to scream, but there was no sound, no release. The darkness pressed in tighter, suffocating his mind as much as his body. The ink, the story, the words—they were alive, and they were wrapping around him, binding him to this place, to this fate. His story was not his own. It never had been.

The whispers grew again, this time taking form—shapes, images, flashes of words and fragments of sentences he couldn't quite grasp. They were dancing just out of his reach, mocking him. His own words, twisted and distorted, swirling around him like a whirlwind, each one a jagged piece of his shattered soul.

"Stop it!" he shouted, his voice weak, ragged. The words felt like a foreign language on his tongue. They had no power. No meaning. He felt as though they were nothing but empty syllables in the face of this insurmountable silence.

"You can't stop it," the voice purred. "You are the story. And the story doesn't end. Not until I say it does."

Evan clutched his chest, gasping for air that wasn't there. His heart pounded, each beat a drum of desperation, of hopelessness. He was drowning in this silence, trapped in a world where the words didn't just speak—they controlled. They consumed.

The silence wasn't empty anymore. It was full of eyes—eyes that stared at him, unblinking, waiting, judging. The darkness wasn't just a void. It was a living thing, a creature that fed on fear and pain, and it was feeding on him.

And then, amidst the chaos of whispers and the weight of the silence, the ink began to bleed. Not on the pages, but from the walls of the room itself, dripping like black liquid, seeping into the cracks of the floor. It was everywhere. It was in him, around him, devouring him.

He reached out, desperate for something solid, but his hands were met with nothing but ink—ink that bled into his skin, ink that swallowed him whole.

"Help me…" he whispered, but even the words felt like a betrayal. A hollow plea that went unanswered.

The darkness surged forward, and with a final, suffocating wave, it enveloped him completely.

And then, there was nothing.

Only the silence. The silence that screamed.

<h1 style="text-align:center">23</h1>

<h1 style="text-align:center">The Pages Turned</h1>

Evan opened his eyes, but this time, the world was different. He was no longer surrounded by darkness or suffocating silence. There was light—bright, harsh light, like the unforgiving glare of a spotlight. He blinked rapidly, trying to adjust, but his vision remained blurry, and his senses still felt dull, as though he had just emerged from the depths of some abyss.

The first thing he noticed was the room. It wasn't the ink-filled void he had just been in. It wasn't even a room, really. It was a long corridor, stretching infinitely in both directions, a hallway made entirely of pale, yellowing paper. It was as if the walls, the floors, even the ceiling, were all one long sheet of paper, worn and faded with age. The paper was delicate, crinkling under his feet as though it might tear at the slightest movement. There were no doors, no windows, just an endless stretch of paper that seemed to go on forever.

Evan felt disoriented. His body moved on autopilot as his mind tried to process the change. He looked down at his hands, still trembling, still stained with the ink. He could still feel it inside him—still hear the whispers, faint but present, in the back of his mind. The words had not let go. They never would.

His heart pounded in his chest. "What is this place?" he whispered to no one in particular, the sound of his own voice unnerving in the stark silence. But as soon as the words left his lips, he knew he wasn't alone.

At the far end of the hallway, he saw something moving. A shadow, indistinct at first, shifting just beyond his reach, barely visible in the dim light. It was too quick to be human, too fluid to be solid. And as it moved closer, it seemed to stretch the very fabric of the paper around it, distorting the edges of the walls. Evan's breath hitched.

His first instinct was to run. He had to get away from whatever was coming toward him. But his legs wouldn't cooperate. They felt like lead, heavy and unresponsive, as though they too had been trapped in this strange, inescapable place. The closer the shadow came, the stronger the feeling that he was being pulled toward it, helpless, drawn into the same vortex that had consumed him before.

Then, the voice came again. But this time, it wasn't just the voice. It was a presence. A force that seemed to wrap around him, saturating the air with its weight.

"Evan..."

The whisper sounded like his own name, but it wasn't his voice.

It was too soft, too menacing, as if the very sound of it was meant to tear him apart. The voice stretched and twisted, curling through the words, slipping through the air like an intangible substance. It made his skin crawl.

He opened his mouth to speak, but nothing came out. The words were trapped in his throat, as though the paper itself was suffocating him.

The shadow grew larger, now fully visible, standing at the end of the hallway, a dark figure clothed in swirling, inky blackness. It was a shape, a silhouette, with no clear features, just a shifting, amorphous form. Evan felt his pulse quicken, his instincts screaming at him to run, but his feet refused to move. He could feel the weight of the paper beneath him, holding him in place.

The figure took a step forward.

The ground beneath Evan's feet cracked, the paper splitting like parchment in the hands of an unseen writer. A violent shudder ran through the air, a tremor that sent ripples through the walls of paper. The shadow moved again, this time faster, its form distorting as it came closer, its presence overwhelming. Every inch it closed, every step it took, Evan felt as if something inside him was being torn apart, unraveling piece by piece.

"You can't escape me, Evan."

The words weren't spoken aloud. They were inside his head, crawling through his thoughts, twisting his mind. It was the voice of the story, the voice of the ink, the voice that had always been there, lurking just behind the words he wrote. The ink had taken over, and now it was alive, feeding on his fear, pulling him deeper into the maze of pages that surrounded him.

The shadow reached out, its form elongating like an arm, stretching toward him with a single clawed hand. Evan staggered backward, but it was too late. The hand touched his shoulder, cold and clammy, the ink spilling from its fingertips, seeping into his skin.

He gasped, his chest tightening as the ink crawled beneath his flesh, like worms burrowing through his veins, poisoning him, consuming him. His vision blurred as the world around him spun.

"You are mine," the voice whispered, and Evan realized with a sickening certainty that the story had always owned him. It had created him, bound him, and now, it was devouring him.

The paper around him began to shift and warp, the ink spilling from the cracks, flooding the hallway in a tidal wave of darkness. The shadow that stood before him began to change, its form shifting into something that Evan recognized all too well—a reflection of himself. His own face, twisted and distorted, stared back at him with empty eyes, a hollow version of himself.

"You can't outrun your own story," the doppelgänger said, its voice a sickening mockery of his own.

Evan recoiled, stumbling backward as the ink began to close in on him. The walls of paper, once fragile, now pulsed with life, folding and shifting like the pages of a book, trapping him in a labyrinth of words and ink.

"This is the end, Evan."

He couldn't breathe, couldn't think. The ink was everywhere now, a suffocating, consuming flood, and the words were closing in around him, binding him to this place, to the story he had never been able to escape. The shadows closed in, and the last thing Evan saw was the face of the doppelgänger grinning at him, its hollow eyes mocking him, before the ink swallowed him whole.

And then, there was nothing.

No words. No story. No light. Only the endless, consuming void of the pages.

24

The Author's Last Penstroke

Evan blinked, gasping for air that didn't seem to exist. His mind was a blur of conflicting thoughts, each one crashing against the other like waves in a storm. His chest heaved as he tried to find his bearings, but everything around him was shifting. The ground beneath him was no longer solid—it was soft, like paper, like it could collapse at any moment.

His hands trembled as he reached out to steady himself, but there was nothing. The room, the world, the very air itself was in motion, swirling around him in chaotic spirals of ink and fragments of words.

"What is this?" His voice was raw, distant, almost alien to him, and yet there was a familiarity to it that made his skin crawl.

The walls around him weren't walls at all—they were pages. Pages that seemed to move and flicker, the ink shifting, the words rearranging themselves like a story still in progress, one that had no end, no resolution. The edges of the pages were torn, frayed, and smeared with dark stains. Ink dripped from the corners, pooling at his feet like blood. And in the middle of it all, there was a single object, lying still, untouched by the chaos.

A pen.

It rested on a table in the center of the room, perfectly pristine amidst the madness. But it was no ordinary pen. It was heavy, ancient-looking, and its sleek black surface gleamed in the half-light. Evan felt an odd pull toward it, a magnetic force that seemed to call to him. The very air seemed to grow still as he took a step toward the table, his feet dragging as if the ground itself didn't want him to approach.

His fingers brushed the pen's smooth surface, and the moment his skin made contact, the world around him stilled. The flickering ink paused, the shifting words froze. The air, once thick with a tangible weight of oppression, seemed to clear, but it was not a relief. No, it was worse. It was anticipation.

Evan's breath quickened as the pen seemed to come alive beneath his fingertips, warm, pulsating with an almost sinister energy. He picked it up, the weight of it more than just physical. It felt like the pen was waiting—waiting for him to write, to begin, to finish.

The voice came again, this time without warning, echoing through his mind, inside his very bones.

"You think you can control it now?"

Evan froze, the pen hovering inches above the page in front of him. The room, once disorienting, now seemed like a stage, the table like a platform on which everything—his fate, his soul, his life—was to be decided. The voice, familiar and distant all at once, slithered through his mind. "You're still the writer, Evan. But now, you've run out of pages."

He turned, eyes searching the empty corners of the room, but no one was there. The room felt more like a tomb than a place of creation, the walls bearing the weight of centuries of stories, of lives lived and lost within them. The words—his words—were scattered everywhere like debris, and there, at the center of it all, lay the pen, the final instrument of his undoing.

"I—I don't understand," Evan whispered, his voice trembling.

The pen clicked once, a sharp, final sound that resonated through the silence. The ink began to move again, faster this time, as though it had been waiting for this moment. Evan felt it before he saw it—the paper in front of him rippled, as though the story itself was coming alive, rising from the page like a living thing, hungry for completion.

"You think you're different?" The voice was now a whisper, so close it was as if it was inside his mind. "You can't escape what you are. You are the story."

A rush of panic filled Evan's chest, his breath coming in shallow gasps. His grip on the pen tightened as the ink on the page began to take form. Figures, shadows, shapes, all began to emerge from the words. They were his creations. His characters. But they weren't just figures anymore—they were real. They were coming for him.

The air grew heavy, charged with electricity, the ink forming into tendrils that twisted and writhed like serpents. His characters—his creations—were breaking free from the confines of the story, their forms becoming more and more solid as the ink poured from the page, spilling over the edge, oozing into the air like liquid darkness. Each character, a mirror of his own soul, approached him with eyes full of accusation, with faces twisted in anger, fear, and betrayal.

"You wrote us," one of them whispered, its voice cold, hollow. "And now we want more."

Evan stumbled back, but the room wouldn't let him. The pages rose from the floor like waves crashing toward him, trapping him, hemming him in with no way out. The characters—the creations of his own mind—surrounded him, their eyes glowing with an eerie light.

"You wrote the ending," the voice echoed, louder now. "But you can't escape it. It's already been written. And now, you will live it."

Evan's heart raced as the figures closed in, their forms solidifying, becoming more real with every passing second. He could feel their cold eyes on him, their every movement reverberating through his chest. The room seemed to be shrinking, the walls pressing in closer, the floor beneath him buckling and shifting with each breath he took.

His mind raced. He had to write. He had to finish the story, but the pressure was unbearable. The pen felt impossibly heavy now, as though it were pulling him down, pulling him into the page itself. The ink swirled around him like a flood, closing in, suffocating him. His pulse pounded in his ears as he tried to push the pen down, but his hand was frozen.

The voice of the story spoke again, its words a low, guttural murmur. "You've always been the one to write the endings, Evan. But this time... you can't."

The last of the figures—his own reflection, now twisted and deformed—stepped forward. It smiled, a horrible, empty grin.

"You're the story now," it whispered.

Evan's mind snapped.

The pen hit the paper with a violent crack.

And then everything stopped.

The room, the ink, the characters—all froze in place. A deafening silence rang in his ears. For a brief, terrifying moment, everything felt still. Too still. Evan could feel his heartbeat in his throat, the weight of the silence pressing against him like a tangible force.

He looked down at the page.

The ink had dried. The words had settled. There were no

more pages left to turn. No more twists, no more unfinished sentences. No more stories to write.

Evan slowly lowered the pen, his hand trembling. His breath hitched in his chest as he realized the truth.

The story was finished.

And he... was no longer the author.

25

The Writer's Ghost

Evan woke to the sound of his own breath, ragged and shallow, as if the very air had been stolen from his lungs. His eyes snapped open, but the world around him was still dark, suffocatingly so. His vision adjusted slowly, but no matter how hard he tried to focus, the scene around him remained elusive, like a memory just out of reach.

He was lying on something soft—no, too soft—like paper. The surface beneath him crinkled when he shifted, and he could feel the texture under his fingertips. Something wet and cold brushed against his hand, and he pulled back sharply, sitting up with a jolt.

It was ink.

Thick, black ink had pooled around him, staining the floor, the walls, and creeping into the air itself. The oppressive weight of it was suffocating, as if the very ink that had once filled his pages was now suffocating him, binding him to the space, pulling him into the depths of the story. It felt as though he were drowning in it, and the more he struggled, the thicker it became, wrapping tighter around him, clinging to his skin, his lungs, his heart.

A cold chill ran down his spine as he looked around. The walls of the room—if it could even be called that—seemed to be made of paper, too. Thin, yellowed pages stretched endlessly, folding over each other like a sea of forgotten words. They were crumpled in places, torn in others, but all of them had one thing in common: they were blank.

The ink, the ink everywhere... it was as if the story had been erased, leaving nothing behind but the darkness of the page.

He stood, his legs unsteady beneath him, feeling the cold ink seep into his shoes as if it were trying to pull him down into the ground itself. The darkness in the room seemed to pulse with the rhythm of his heartbeat, thick and oppressive. There were no windows, no doors—just endless paper, endless ink, and an endless silence.

And then, the voice came again.

"Evan..."

It was faint at first, like a whisper caught in the wind, but it grew louder, clearer. It was the same voice—the one that had tormented him since he first began writing, the one that had woven itself into every line, every paragraph, every chapter of his life. It was the voice of the story. The voice of the author.

"You thought you could escape," it said, and Evan felt his blood run cold. "But you can't. Not anymore."

His pulse quickened as the ink began to shift, moving like liquid tendrils creeping along the floor, twisting up the walls, swirling in the air like smoke. It was as if the very fabric of the place—this prison of words—was alive, reacting to his presence. He could hear it now, the rustling of pages, the faint crackling of ink being written, being created. The air was thick with the stench of ink, as if the world around him was being consumed by it.

A shadow moved in the distance. At first, it was nothing more than a flicker at the edge of his vision, but then it began to take shape. Slowly, deliberately. The silhouette of a figure, a tall, thin shape emerging from the ink, stretching and twisting like smoke caught in the wind.

"Evan," the voice purred, closer now. "You never learned, did you?"

He backed away, panic flooding his chest. His mind screamed at him to run, to escape, but there was nowhere to go. The shadow stepped forward, moving with unnatural grace, its shape growing clearer. It was him. It was his reflection, but twisted, contorted, like a broken mirror.

"Why did you write us?" The figure asked, its voice a haunting echo of his own, distorted and cold. "Why did you trap us in your world?"

Evan's heart pounded in his chest as he took another step back. The shadow—his own reflection—was getting closer, its eyes empty, lifeless. The air around him thickened, suffocating him with every breath.

"I—I didn't mean to," Evan stammered, his words falling apart as he tried to explain, to make sense of everything. But the shadow didn't wait for him to finish.

It reached out, long fingers stretching, and Evan could feel it— the pull. The need. The compulsion to reach out, to take the shadow's hand, to let it lead him into the unknown, into the place where stories ended, and there was nothing left but ink.

"You can't escape us, Evan," the reflection said, its voice low, almost soothing. "We are you. We are everything you've ever written."

Evan shook his head violently, trying to break free from the grip of the words, the pull of the ink. But the figure was already too close, its fingers brushing his shoulder like ice. The moment it touched him, everything shifted.

The world around him flickered, a series of images flashing in his mind. Scenes. Pages. Chapters. All of it—every story he had written, every word he had spilled onto the paper—began to crash together, colliding like a thousand pieces of shattered glass. He saw faces, names, places—his characters, his stories, all of them swirling around him like a storm.

The pen.

It was in his hand again, the same heavy, cursed pen that had once been his salvation, and now, it felt like a chain, binding him to this place, to the endless page. His hand trembled as he raised it, the tip of the pen hovering over the blank space before him. But this time, it wasn't the act of creation that terrified him—it was the act of destruction.

"You can't write your way out of this," the shadow whispered, its voice coming from every direction at once. "You created us, but now we own you."

Evan's eyes widened as he realized the truth—the terrifying, inescapable truth.

He wasn't the creator anymore. He wasn't the writer. He was the character, trapped in his own story. The ink, the pages, the words—they had all come alive, and now they were closing in on him, suffocating him, consuming him.

The shadow moved closer still, and Evan felt the finality of it. The words had already been written. The ending had been decided long ago.

There was no escape.

And then, as the ink swirled around him, pulling him into its depths, he heard the voice one last time, low and final:

"You are the story now."

And everything went dark.

26

The Final Paragraph

Evan's heart thudded loudly in his chest, the pulse echoing in his ears like a drumbeat. The ink around him seemed to thicken, stretching up like dark tendrils, reaching for him with a mind of its own. He felt his skin crawl, the weight of the ink sinking into him, pressing on his body from every direction. Every breath was a battle, as the air grew thick and suffocating, laced with the scent of old paper and decay. His hands shook uncontrollably, the pen still clenched tightly in his grasp. It felt like the weight of the entire world was pressing down on him, trying to force him into submission, trying to make him write again.

But Evan couldn't.

His fingers hovered over the page, the blankness mocking him. The words he had once controlled—once created—were now nothing more than echoes in the dark. The characters, the places, the stories... they had all bled together, merging into one chaotic mess that had consumed everything. There was no escape. No way out.

And yet, something deep inside him refused to give in.

He looked around, the walls of the paper prison closing in, the room spinning. There was no door, no window, no exit of any kind. The only thing that existed in this twisted place was the pen and the endless pages that stretched on forever. The shadow of himself, his reflection, stood watching him, its hollow eyes full of dark amusement, waiting for him to make his move.

"You can't run from this, Evan," the shadow said, its voice cold and final. "It's your story. You wrote it. You created it, and now you have to live it."

Evan swallowed hard, the words sinking into his bones like poison. It was true, wasn't it? He had written this. He had trapped himself in the narrative, penned his own fate with every line, every paragraph. He had been the master of the words, the creator of worlds—but now, he was nothing more than a prisoner of his own making.

His reflection grinned, the expression twisting into something grotesque. It took a step forward, its movements unnervingly smooth.

"You always wanted control," it whispered, the voice like a caress. "But control is a lie, Evan. You can't control the story once it's been written. You can't control the ending."

Evan's pulse quickened as the ink around him started to churn, the liquid seeping into his clothes, into his very skin, like it was trying to drown him, to erase him completely. He wanted to scream, to fight, but his throat was dry, his voice stuck in his chest. He couldn't move. He couldn't think. It was as if every part of him was being consumed by the story, swallowed whole by the ink that had once been his lifeblood.

And then, just as everything seemed to fade to black, the pen in his hand seemed to pull him. Not physically, but mentally. A force, almost magnetic, tugged at his mind. The words, his own words, began to rise in his thoughts, one by one, like a chant, a hypnotic lullaby.

The end. The end. The end.

The words repeated in his mind, over and over, louder with each passing second. It was the end of the story. The end of the book. The end of him.

"Don't," he whispered, his voice hoarse, barely a sound. "Please, don't make me write it."

The shadow tilted its head, the grin widening, its voice deepening. "You have no choice. It's already been written. You were always going to be here. Always going to be trapped."

Evan closed his eyes, the weight of the ink around him threatening to crush him. But even in the face of his own doom, a spark of defiance flickered inside him. No. He would not give in. He could not. Not like this. Not after everything.

With every ounce of strength he had left, Evan squeezed the pen tighter, his fingers raw from the pressure, the ink dripping from its tip like blood. He refused to be a part of this story. He refused to be the final chapter.

Think, Evan. Think!

He took a step forward, pushing through the ink, his feet sinking into it with each movement. His body screamed in protest, but he kept going. The shadow, his reflection, was still there, watching, waiting. But Evan didn't stop. He couldn't. Not when he was so close.

He reached out, his hand shaking, and touched the nearest page. The paper was cold, rough, the ink smeared and dark, but he didn't care. He wasn't going to let this be his end. He wasn't going to let the ink consume him.

With one final, desperate movement, Evan brought the pen to the page. His hand moved of its own accord, the tip of the pen scratching against the surface, forming letters, words—words that had been buried deep in his mind. He couldn't control it. He couldn't stop it. But he wasn't writing the ending. No, he was writing something else.

A new story.

The ink began to spread, but it wasn't black anymore. It was white—pure, blindingly bright, like light spilling from the tip of the pen. The pages around him began to glow, the ink seeping through the cracks of his broken world, illuminating the darkness. The walls of the paper prison trembled, the weight of the words shifting.

"You think you can rewrite it?" The shadow laughed, its voice echoing with disdain. "You think you can change the end?"

Evan's eyes burned as the ink continued to spread, the words flowing faster, faster, faster until they filled every corner of the room. It was a flood, a tidal wave of light and power. The shadow's voice became a distant hum, fading as the pages were consumed by the bright ink, until nothing remained but the glowing words, the new story that Evan had created.

He collapsed to his knees, his breath coming in ragged gasps. The pen fell from his hand, the glow slowly fading as the words settled, the story complete. He had done it. He had rewritten it. The ending was no longer the end. The darkness, the ink, the shadow—they were gone.

For the first time in what felt like an eternity, Evan opened his eyes fully, the world around him quiet and still. The pages, now pristine and blank, surrounded him. The ink had vanished. There was no more weight, no more pressure. The story was over.

Or... was it just beginning?

27

The Unwritten Truth

Evan's fingers twitched as he stood, staring at the blank pages surrounding him. The light was still dim, the soft glow from his rewriting fading slowly, retreating into the corners like a memory that would soon be forgotten. The ink had disappeared, leaving only the untouched, pristine white of paper. There was an eerie stillness in the air, as if the world had paused in the aftermath of the storm, waiting for something—or someone— to break the silence.

But Evan knew one thing for certain: the fight wasn't over. No, this—this moment—was just the calm before the real storm. He could feel it in his bones, the cold certainty settling over him like a shroud. It wasn't over. Not by a long shot.

He took a tentative step forward, the creak of his shoes the only sound in the vast, empty room. His breath felt shallow, as if the air was growing thinner around him, but he couldn't shake the sensation that he wasn't alone. No, not alone—watched. He wasn't sure when the feeling started, but it had crept up on him, growing with each passing second until it had consumed him entirely.

And then, he heard it.

A faint rustling. The whisper of pages turning.

Evan froze, his body rigid, his pulse spiking. He whipped his head around, trying to pinpoint the source of the noise, but the room remained eerily silent, the blank pages hanging in the air like vultures waiting to descend. His eyes darted to the corner of the room, to the far wall, where there was nothing but more paper. Empty. Unwritten.

But there was something about that wall. Something about the way the shadows clung to it, how they seemed to stretch and writhe, like they were alive.

The rustling came again, louder this time.

Evan took a cautious step back, his heart thudding painfully in his chest. His eyes widened in horror as the shadows on the wall began to shift. It wasn't just the shadows that moved; it was the pages themselves. They twitched, like the room was alive, the paper stirring, bending at the corners as if it were trying to escape its own imprisonment.

Without thinking, Evan bolted for the nearest exit, but there was none. There had been no door, no window, no way out—just endless, endless paper. He turned back, his breath coming in desperate gasps, and that's when he saw it.

A figure.

The same figure he had seen before. The shadow. The one that had tormented him from the very beginning. But this time, it wasn't just a reflection of his own form—it was more than that. The figure was real. It stepped forward, its movement fluid, unnatural, as if it were born from the very paper itself.

Evan's throat tightened. The figure—his reflection—was smiling. That same twisted grin that had haunted his every thought, his every word, now spread across its face, stretching wider, more unnerving. It wasn't just a shadow. It was alive, and it knew him—too well.

"You thought you could rewrite the ending," the figure said, its voice dripping with malice. "But the truth is... you don't control the story. Not anymore."

Evan's hand flew to his chest, his heart racing as the figure took another step forward. The room seemed to shrink around him, the walls closing in, the paper shifting like the weight of the story was pressing down on him, squeezing the very air from his lungs. He couldn't breathe. Couldn't think.

The figure reached out, its long, twisted fingers extending toward him.

"No," Evan whispered, his voice barely audible. "I—I can still fight. I can still change it."

The figure's grin widened, its eyes glowing with an unnatural light. "There is no changing this, Evan. The ending has always been written, you just didn't see it."

Evan stumbled back, his mind spinning, the weight of those words crashing down on him. What did it mean? What was the ending? The truth that had been hidden from him all this time?

His eyes darted to the pages again, the blank paper stretching endlessly in every direction. The words were still there, buried deep in his mind, waiting to be revealed. Waiting to be written. The truth.

The rustling came again, this time from the walls. The pages shifted violently, as if they were coming alive, unfolding like some monstrous creature, the creases and folds revealing what was hidden beneath.

And then Evan saw it.

A word. One word, written in bold, jagged letters, appearing at the center of the wall. It was distorted, almost as if it was trying to escape, the ink not yet fully settled, like it had just been scrawled by a hand that was too eager to finish.

THE END.

Evan's breath caught in his throat. No. This couldn't be the end. This couldn't be the truth.

The figure laughed, a low, hollow sound that echoed through the room. "The truth was there all along. You just refused to see it."

"No," Evan said, shaking his head, trying to push the words away. "This isn't the end. I won't let it be the end."

He took a step toward the wall, reaching out with trembling hands to tear at the word, to erase it, to change it, but before his fingers could touch the paper, the figure lunged.

It was too fast. Too powerful. The shadow wrapped around Evan, suffocating him, engulfing him in its cold, inky embrace. He tried to scream, but no sound escaped his mouth. He couldn't breathe. He couldn't see. He was lost in the dark, tangled in the very fabric of the story.

And then, through the chaos, he heard the voice again, the voice that had started it all.

"You can't change it, Evan. You were never meant to. It was always going to end like this. The story was written long before you ever picked up the pen."

Evan felt the last of his strength fade as the figure pulled him deeper into the darkness. The ink consumed him, the words wrapping around him like chains, pulling him toward the truth he had refused to face.

And then, just as his vision blurred, the last thing he saw was that word. The End.

But this time, it wasn't just the end of the story. It was the end of him.

28

The Echo of the Beginning

The darkness pressed against Evan, suffocating him in its endless grip. He was no longer sure where he was, or even who he was. His body felt like a distant memory, his thoughts hazy, as if the very essence of him had been wiped away by the shadow's grip. There was only the suffocating void, the whisper of ink and paper, and the haunting echo of that single word: *The End.*

But even as his mind struggled to hold onto anything solid, a flicker of awareness sparked inside him, a faint memory of something. Something... *before.*

Before the ink. Before the pages had become his prison. Before he had written himself into this twisted fate.

Evan inhaled sharply, his lungs burning as he tried to regain some sense of control. It felt as though time had collapsed in on itself, the seconds stretching into infinity, and yet somehow, there was a glimmer of something. A light. A distant sound.

The rustling. A sound of paper moving, pages turning, not in the way they had before, but with purpose. It wasn't random. It was deliberate. A slow turning, as if a reader was flipping through the chapters of a book, each page a step closer to something that had yet to be revealed.

His eyes fluttered open—or at least, he thought they did. The darkness around him shifted, breaking apart, like a web being undone, and for the first time in what felt like forever, Evan saw *light*. Not the blinding white of before, but a soft, warm glow, like sunlight filtering through a crack in a long-forgotten door.

He wasn't sure how, but his legs moved. He didn't know if he was walking or floating, but he was *moving*. Every step felt heavy, like the weight of the entire world was on his shoulders, but he couldn't stop now. He couldn't. There was something— *someone*—he needed to find.

The pages shifted again, this time much closer, as if the words themselves were waiting for him to return. He reached out instinctively, his fingers grazing against the edges of the paper, and he was struck by a sudden flood of memory. Not just the words of his story, but the sensation of *writing* them. Of creating them. He remembered the satisfaction of the first line, the excitement of the characters coming to life, the *control* he had once felt.

But now... that control had slipped through his fingers, like sand, and the weight of his decisions had crushed him under their force.

And then, the room shifted again.

The walls—made of paper, crumbling paper—were falling away, leaving him standing in the center of a vast, open space. The light grew brighter, warmer, until it filled the room entirely. And there, standing in the middle of it all, was a figure. One he recognized immediately.

Her.

Lily.

She stood there, framed by the light, her silhouette a perfect contrast against the glow. Her long hair shimmered like threads of gold, her eyes wide, searching, waiting. She was still as beautiful as the day he had first met her, but there was something different now. Something more.

Something *familiar.*

"Lily..." he whispered, his voice hoarse from the darkness, barely a sound. "Is it really you?"

She didn't answer right away. Instead, she stepped forward, the light following her, wrapping around her like an embrace. She moved toward him slowly, deliberately, as though every step was a decision. But there was no fear in her eyes—only the soft, knowing gaze of someone who had always known this moment was coming.

"You've been lost for so long, Evan," she said softly, her voice like a melody, clear and steady. "But now, you're here. You've found your way back."

Evan's breath caught in his throat, the sound of her voice stirring something deep inside him. His chest tightened with the weight of her words, but he couldn't make sense of them. "Found my way back?" he repeated, his voice trembling. "But... how? I—I thought you were gone. I thought I—"

"You thought you were alone," she said, cutting him off gently, her gaze never leaving his. "But you were never alone, Evan. You've been writing your way to me all along. Every word, every page, every twist in the story—was leading you back to this moment."

His mind reeled as her words sank in. *Writing your way to me.* The realization hit him like a jolt of electricity, sharp and sudden. She wasn't just a character. No. She was more than that. She had always been more than that. She was the key, the anchor that had tied him to this world, the one piece of the story that had kept him grounded, even when the ink threatened to consume him whole.

But it didn't make sense. How had she known? How had she been *waiting* for him?

"I don't understand," Evan said, stepping closer to her, his confusion clear. "How could you know? You... you were just a character in my story. A figment of my imagination."

Lily's expression softened, a small, knowing smile curling at the corners of her lips. "No, Evan. I'm more than that. And so are you. You've always been. You created me, yes—but you didn't just create me. You created *us*. And that's where the story always began. *Together*. You and I."

Evan's heart raced, the weight of her words hitting him with a force he couldn't explain. The pieces, once scattered and fragmented, were starting to fall into place. There was a connection here—a bond—that transcended the lines of his writing, the boundaries of his imagination. She wasn't just the woman he had written about. She was the one who had been *written into* him.

And in that moment, everything about the story—the ink, the words, the pages, the shadow—began to make sense. The truth that had been hidden from him, the truth he had refused to see, was not just about the ending of the story. It was about the beginning.

He had never been alone. He had never been in control.

The story had always been theirs to write together.

With that realization, the last of the shadows lifted from his chest, and for the first time, Evan felt light. Free. As though the very air around him had been waiting for him to take that final step into the light.

Lily reached out for his hand, her fingers brushing his. The contact was like a spark, igniting something deep within him. She smiled, her eyes filled with an emotion he couldn't quite name.

"You've found it, Evan. You've found the truth."

And as her hand closed around his, the world around them began to shift again, the pages turning, the ink flowing—this time, not as a prison, but as a canvas. The beginning. The start of something new. Their story. Together.

The echo of the beginning.

29

The Final Word

The moment Evan grasped Lily's hand, something inside him shattered. The world around him, once defined by rigid pages and unyielding ink, began to bend and twist. The light surrounding them pulsed, shifting in a rhythmic dance, each beat like the sound of a heartbeat, slow but undeniable.

Evan didn't know what was happening, but he felt it. He felt the change in his very bones, the rush of energy surging through his veins. The air crackled with the sensation of something unfolding, something vast and untold, and for the first time in what seemed like forever, the heavy weight of the story lifted from his shoulders.

Lily's touch was like fire, searing and alive. The warmth spread from her fingers into his, racing up his arm, and with it came a flood of memories—his childhood, the first stories he had ever written, the early mornings when the words had flowed effortlessly from his mind. He remembered the first time he had put pen to paper, how it had felt like the beginning of a journey, a grand adventure.

But now, as he stood beside Lily, he realized that journey

had never ended. The adventure had always been there, quietly waiting for him to see it, to acknowledge it. They had never been alone in this.

"You've written yourself into the story," Lily said, her voice soft, almost as if she were speaking to herself, though Evan heard her clearly. "You've always been part of it."

Evan swallowed hard, his mind racing. "What do you mean? What's happening? I—I thought I was done. I thought it was over."

The words hung in the air between them, heavy and charged with an unspoken truth. Lily's gaze softened, and she looked at him as though seeing him for the first time. "There is no ending, Evan. Not the way you think."

The room began to pulse again, and this time, Evan felt it—a deep, resonant thrum, almost like the vibration of a bell. He closed his eyes for a second, feeling the world around him shift, the edges of his vision blurring. When he opened them again, he wasn't sure what had changed, but everything felt... different.

The walls, made of paper and ink, had begun to disappear. The pages he had once written were no longer confined to the room. They stretched outward, spiraling into the unknown, filling the void with words that floated in the air like stars scattered across the heavens.

Evan's heart raced. He knew, with an unsettling certainty, that the story was not over. It had only just begun. But the question was: *who was writing it now?*

As the words took form in front of them, he realized that they weren't his words. Not entirely. They were his thoughts, his emotions, his fears, but they had taken on a life of their own, moving beyond his control, beyond even his understanding. The words shifted and twisted, each phrase seeming to write itself, as if some unseen hand were guiding the narrative.

The words... they were writing *him.*

Evan's breath hitched. "What is this? What's happening to me?"

"You're being rewritten," Lily said, her voice steady, as if she had known this moment would come. "The story was always fluid, Evan. You can't hold it in place forever. You're part of it, but it's part of you too. And now it's time for the next chapter."

A shiver ran down Evan's spine. He could feel it now—the words pressing against him, pulling at the edges of his existence, trying to shape him into something else. But he was no longer sure who or what he was meant to be. The line between creator and creation had blurred beyond recognition, and for the first time, Evan realized he didn't have control over the story anymore.

It was as though his entire identity was crumbling under the weight of the words that had once flowed from his pen. The pressure built, the ink in the air swirling faster, more erratic, until the room seemed to pulse with the rhythm of it all. The story was alive, and it was rewriting him. It was rewriting them.

"No," Evan gasped, his voice shaking. "I can't... I don't know who I am anymore. I don't know what's real."

Lily's eyes softened. She stepped closer, her presence grounding him in the chaos, her hand still clutched tightly in his. "You don't have to know everything, Evan. The story is bigger than you, bigger than me. But you *are* real. You're always going to be real. You always were."

He wanted to believe her. But the uncertainty gnawed at him. The boundaries were eroding, the lines between his reality and the world of the story blurring beyond recognition. He was being pulled in two directions—one toward the world he had written, and the other toward something new, something unknown.

The final word had yet to be written, and Evan couldn't stop it. He couldn't stop *any* of it.

And then, the words stopped moving.

The room fell silent. Everything, for a moment, stood still, as if the world itself were holding its breath.

A single page floated before Evan, suspended in midair. It was blank—utterly blank—except for one thing. One word. One sentence that had taken form at the top of the page. It was written in ink, bold and dark, the letters sharp and clear:

The End.

Evan's heart stopped. He reached for the page, his fingers trembling as he touched it, the ink cold against his skin. His breath caught in his throat as he stared at the word. The one word that had haunted him from the very beginning. The word that had been his curse.

But as his fingers traced the edges of the page, something shifted. The word began to fade. The ink started to blur, melting into the air like smoke. It dissolved, vanishing into the vast emptiness, leaving nothing behind but the feeling of *possibility*.

The word was gone. But the story wasn't over.

Evan looked at Lily, her face illuminated by the soft, golden glow of the light around them. She was still there, still beside him, and for the first time, he felt a sense of peace. A sense of *belonging*. The story, whatever it had been, was not his alone. It had never been just his. It had always been *theirs*.

And as the words of the story swirled in the air, reformed, and began to take new shape, Evan realized the truth:

There was no final word.

Not as long as the story was still being written.